Probing the Mind of a Serial Killer

Jack A. Apsche

Foreword by
A. Charles Peruto, Jr., Esq.

NORMAN F. BOURKE
MEMORIAL LIBRARY
CAYUGA COMMUNITY
COLLEGE
AUBURN, NEW YORK 13021

International Information
Associates, Inc.
Morrisville, PA

Library of Congress Number 93-77078

Apsche, Jack A.

Probing the Mind of a Serial Killer

ISBN 0-945510-12-8

Copyright © 1993

International Information Associates, Inc.

ALL RIGHTS RESERVED

Neither this book, nor any part may be reproduced or transmitted in any form, or by any means electronic or mechanical, including photocopying, microfilming, or recording, or by any information or retrieval system [beyond that copying permitted in Sections 107 & 108 of the U.S. copyright law, and except by reviewers of the public or academic press] without written permission of the publisher.

International Information Associates, Inc.
P.O. Box 773, Morrisville, PA 19067 U.S.A.

Current Printing [last digit]
10 9 8 7 6 5 4 3 2 1

Printed in the United States of America

DEDICATION

This book is dedicated to Robert K. Ressler. We would still be standing near, and "looking into the abyss" without his pioneering effort. Thank you Mr. Ressler.

THANKS STUFF...

It seems appropriate to thank those people who, in a variety of ways, allowed this book to be completed. So, thank you, one and all.

Included among these "thank you's" are my daughter, Melissa, who thinks that "it's cool," and my son, Joey, who just wanted to see it done.

An especially big thanks goes to my wife, Joanne, who had to live through all the phases of this work, and the writing of the book —and she's still married to me! Thank you, I love you.

Finally, thanks to Richard Bradley. Without his belief in this project, and because of his guidelines, we were able to complete it. You were right, "there was a book in there somewhere." I hope I found it.

Finally, it is my hope that this book contributes to continued research and understanding into the phenomena of serial killers. As such, I thank you, the reader of this book.

Table of Contents

FOREWORD

PREFACE

SOME HISTORICAL & LEGAL CONSIDERATIONS 1

THE DIAGNOSTIC CATEGORY OF SERIAL KILLER 9

CHARACTERISTICS OF A SERIAL KILLER 9

FANTASY: THE BEGINNING 31

THE BEGINNINGS IN HEIDNIK'S WORDS 32

KIDNAPPING & RAPE: A WARNING 39

THE FANTASY IS THE MOTIVE 53

VICTIM SELECTION 63

THE MANIPULATOR 75

SUICIDE AND CONTROL 101

INTIMACY, BONDING AND CONTROL 112

A FUNCTIONAL ANALYSIS OF THE BEHAVIOR 135

EPILOGUE 142

APPENDIXES 143

BIBLIOGRAPHY 222

THE AUTHOR:

Jack Apsche holds a doctorate in Psychological Studies from Temple University in Philadelphia. He is currently pursuing an advanced degree in Criminal Justice. Dr. Apsche is a researcher, author, lecturer, and consultant. His curiosity in human behavior extends well beyond serial killers, from the everyday problems of everyday people, to the particular problems of Viet Nam veterans, the behavior of organized crime and law enforcement, and the rise of the German neo-Nazi movement. His research centers on the quest to uncover the reasons for the behavior differences between the "saints," the "sinners," and the rest of us.

Dr. Apsche lives with his wife and family in Levittown, PA.

Foreword

You may wonder why an attorney is writing a foreword for a psychology text, but the sanity or insanity of serial murderers is an important legal issue. In fact, whether or not a person is insane is not a mental health issue at all, it is a legal judgment. Acknowledged mentally ill individuals, even those who have committed unimaginable serial or ritualistic murders, are not necessarily insane under the law.

Think about it. When you hear about a serial killing, and see and hear just part of the actual details of these events from the all - pervasive TV network news, your first reaction is that the killer is insane. You'd have to be "crazy" to even think of the things that were done! But, those killings are frightening, horrifying and, at the same time, somewhat compelling. The media knows this and plays to all these feelings.

How could anyone in their right mind do such terrifying things to another human being? It's hard to understand the motive. For mental health professionals, law enforcement, judges, attorneys, and juries understanding the motive is a problem. This lack of understanding allows severely mentally ill individuals to slip in and out of mental health care for years — even decades, until it is too late and the killing begins. It makes apprehension of these individuals by law enforcement difficult, because the motive is missing — at least to the "normal" individual. And once brought into court, judges, juries and attorneys, still not understanding, but knowing the killer must be crazy become entangled in a legal definition over 150 years old!

Part of the problem is the shock at the grotesque details of the actions and the need for society to rid itself of this particular menace. The serial killer, as you will see, is generally extremely intelligent and appears to behave, and answer questions rationally. In fact, most are always helpful and have learned to tell you what you most want to hear. But the world that exists only in their head almost never appears.

Popular culture, books, movies and TV shows portray the serial killer in his external image only. The character never appears crazy but pursues the relentless killing path in a logical rational manner. There's no wild-eyed madman as is often portrayed by actors like Jack Nicholson but a calm, reasoning killer trying to outsmart the system. This is also what happens in real life. But as Dr. Apsche points out in this book, the serial killer lives an internal fantasy world that cannot be seen or understood by those who see him. Juries are then easily manipulated to change their gut feel of insane to sane when confronted by the archaic definition, and the authority of a judge.

This book begins the discovery of the inner world of the serial killer. It shows these individuals to have had mental problems that were being treated for years. It shows how the intelligence of these individuals get them released from institutions over and over again. Released until their fantasies take complete control and are acted out. And once successfully acted out, these powerful fantasies and the feelings of control become stronger and stronger leading to further killings.

To understand this in the detail presented by Jack Apsche, often using the words of an actual serial killer can help society better than all the death penalties and life-in-prison sentences ever can. Knowing what to look for, how to find and understand the fantasy motive, can help law enforcement personnel find these people quicker. Our legal system, juries, attorneys and judges, can then interpret the law in a manner to help society by placing these insane killers in a secure place where they can be studied and helped. They can't be cured, but they can help us understand the disease and help prevent future crimes from being committed.

Perhaps most importantly is the acknowledgment by mental health professionals—psychiatrists and psychologists — that the serial killer is an unrecognized mental health illness. As Dr. Apsche points out these individuals exhibit many of the more traditional and recognized forms of mental illness, but the whole is more than the sum. As the research continues on from the beginnings presented in this book, the serial/ritualistic killer category will become better defined, understood and accepted. Then these people can be reached, confined and treated when they first are admitted for mental health care, not waiting for the victims to be found years later. This book cannot bring back the victims, or console their families and friend. Neither can it prevent these crimes from taking place in the future — at least not by itself. But Dr. Apsche's work offers the first insight and plan for further work that will begin to control the centuries' old horrifying crime — the serial killing.

A. Charles Peruto, Jr.
Philadelphia, Pennsylvania

PREFACE

John 3:20: For everyone who does wicked things hates the light and does not come toward the light, so that his works might not be exposed.

—one of Gary Heidnik's favorite Bible passages.

Although so called serial or ritualistic murders have probably been around since there was enough human beings to form even the most primitive society, it seems that in the last several decades that the incidents of these horrific crimes has been increasing. In fact, there may have been no significant increase in this type of crime at all [on a per capita basis]. Although impossible to prove, much of the seeming increase, may be nothing more than an increase in awareness of the crimes. Awareness traced to coverage by modern media.

Modern media —television, newspapers, news magazines, and radio—now reports these sorts of crimes almost immediately after they have been discovered. Not only are the reports instantaneous and available to more people now then they ever have been, but they are reported with a graphic detail that brings home the horror of the crime to all who hear or see the news. In addition, advances in psychology, forensic science, and crime detection have identified such crimes for what they are, rather than strange unsolved murders which have filled police files in the past.

The purpose of this book is to present *a view into the mind of the serial killer,* by closely examining one serial killer in particular, Gary M. Heidnik of Philadelphia, Pennsylvania. The book simultaneously examines the insanity plea within the current American legal system. Although this latter is not truly within the realm of psychology, it is impossible to discuss this subject without examining that issue. Perhaps the most important objective of this book is to present new and emerging criteria for insanity; criteria that are not covered under the *diagnostic and statistical Manual III-R* of the American Psychiatric

Association. This new diagnostic criteria should be simply called SERIAL MURDERER.

In support of that diagnostic category the book presents information obtained in the form of data gathered from research and numerous articles in the field. More importantly, specific experimental data supplied by thousands of hours of primary research and interviews with the subject, Gary M. Heidnik. It can be demonstrated, through the sound evidence obtained in the Heidnik research, that the insanity plea as applied today, *does not apply to the ritualistic or serial killer.* In addition, these data will allow us to gain valuable insight into the psychological profile of the serial killer. It is hoped that this profile, and its future refinements and extensions, will help to identify such individuals early enough to prevent these shocking crimes. This book is the result of years of pre- and post-trial research and discovery. What I found in the literature is offered as an eclectic review of current thinking on serial killers. Also presented is the evidence to support the work given in the words of Gary Michael Heidnik, from interviews and personal correspondence. *All letters, transcripts, etc., reproduced on this volume are done so with the spelling, grammar, and syntax of the original preserved.*

My wish is that the book is useful to professionals, as well as the general public. It is time that we all learn what is fact and what is fiction. It is time to separate the truth from myth, and Gary Heidnik from Hannibal Lector.

Finally, I hope that *Probing the Mind of a Serial Killer* moves us a step closer to answers to the questions we all ask about serial killers.

Jack A. Apsche
Levittown, Pennsylvania

CHAPTER 1

SOME HISTORICAL AND LEGAL CONSIDERATIONS REGARDING THE SERIAL KILLER

In the United States today the question of defining insanity has become more of a legal issue than a psychiatric, psychological or mental health question. The forensic psychologist or psychiatrist, armed with modern techniques and a new understanding of the human mind based on decades of research, must still adapt to a 19th Century set of guidelines, the M'Naghten rule.

The M'Naghten rule is based on a 1843 English law case of a Scotsman named Daniel M. M'Naghten. *The rules of insanity established in that case are the same rules observed in one-half of the states in America today almost 150 years later.* It is as if the legal system does not acknowledge any advancement in Psychology or Psychiatry since that time. In simple terms, the M'Naghten rule asks if the defendant understood the nature and quality of the act on which he is being tried. It also asks if (s)he knew the difference between right and wrong with respect to that act.

Another legal definition of insanity is given by the American Law Institute (ALI). The American Law Institute's test of criminal responsibility was adopted by the Court of Appeals for the District of Columbia in the Brauner case. It provides:

> A person is not responsible for criminal conduct if at the time of such conduct, as a result of mental disease or defect, he lacks substantial capacity to appreciate the criminality (wrongfulness) of his conduct to the requirement of the law.

Although this ALI guideline of insanity is far more broad, it remains, at its base, a M'Naghten definition of insanity.

There have been major gains through scientific research in the collective fields of mental health since the 1800's. Yet the profession must submit to a out-of-date legalistic and often confining definition of insanity when such matters come before a judicial system in the United States. Significantly, these definitions do *not* apply to some of the most heinous crimes that we face in America today. These are the crimes which capture newspaper headlines and make sensational movies, but seldom if ever do the stories portrayed go beyond the sensationalism to seriously examine the individuals, and the pathology of these individuals.

Often in court cases where insanity is the defense, the prosecution, as well as the defense attorneys, retain a psychiatrist to examine the defendant and give their perspective points of view. In most cases, the retained professionals adopt the point of view of those who retain them.

At the very least, legal professionals have been able to identify those psychiatrists whose views match either a prosecution or defense posture. Quick results may be good law, but is often less than perfect psychiatry or psychology. The problem being is that what is received are several well-educated and often re-

nown but differing opinions of the sanity of the defendant.

Based on different sets of information, and on examinations based on different sets of rules, it is not hard to understand these diversion opinions. Such examinations do not (and neither are they intended) lead to a better understanding of what causes the creation of such a state of mind. It is important, particularly in the case of the ritualistic serial killer, that one looks at the entire history of the individual and thoroughly researches any serial killers also then in captivity. If this examination is done carefully, in a longitudinal manner, there are patterns that emerge relative to this personality as a class.

Before enumerating the characteristics of serial killers, an important point of reference is to review the current categorizations of mass murders, and a brief history of serial killers. Mass murderers have been categorized by many in the past. Mass murderers were compartmentalized into four major groups by Park Dietz, a forensic psychiatrist. Serial murderers, a subcategory of these mass murderers also has its own categorization system. This was also developed by Park Dietz. The serial murder categories were further defined by Richard Rappaport, another forensic psychiatrist.

The categories of mass murderers are as follows:

- Pseudo-commandos
- Family Annihilators
- Set and Run Killers
- Serial Murderers

For the purpose of this study, only the final category of Serial Murderers will be examined. The five categories of serial killer delineated by Doctors Dietz and Rappaport are the following:

- Crime Spree Killers
- Functionaries of Organized Criminal Operations
- Custodial Poisoners and Asphyxiators
- Psychotic
- Sexual Saddest.

The *Crime Spree Killers* are exactly what the term signifies. They are individuals or partners who murder while involved in the commission of other felonies such as bank robberies, illegal drugs, and burglaries.

Functionaries of Organized Criminal Operations usually refers to those who commit murder for profit and/or business motives. These murderers are often associated with the so-called mafia and other contract murderers. Today, many are a part of international drug cartels.

Custodial Poisoners and Asphyxiators are often members of the medical profession. These individuals may murder their patients for financial reasons, or to relieve themselves of the duty of caring for "dependent, debilitated, demanding and helpless patients."

The *Psychotic* category describes a group of individuals known for irrational thinking that often leads to dangerous behaviors. They are often reacting to commands to kill from voices of others within their own head. Many psychotics have religious conflicts and they act on commands from God or the Devil.

The group of killers known as *Sexual Saddest* are marked by the characteristic violation and torture of their victims *prior to the actual murder*. These killers are often identified as white males in their 20's and 30's. They are usually also intelligent, successful, and often have no prior criminal record.

The research which forms the basis of this study clearly

shows that the psychotic and the sexual saddest behavior *interact* in the *Serial Murderer* providing the basis of a new profile. This profile is more than simply the combination of the psychotic and sexual sadist categories. It should be noted that the categories of psychotic and sexual saddest may represent sound criteria for an individual serial murderer. Research conducted on Gary Heidnik (and to a lesser extent with another convicted serial killer, Harrison Graham) and others, suggests that *a bridge of both categories may exist in the serial killer.*

Along with such categorization schemes, it is equally important to have a sense of historical prospective regarding the serial killers. Elliott Leyton in his book *Hunting Humans* provides an excellent overview of the history of serial murder. Although this book is predominantly a socioanthropological view of the problem it is an excellent source for obtaining this historical perspective.

Included in this book by some of the more infamous, but perhaps not so well-known serial killers of the past. These include:

- Sawney Beam, the 15th Century Scot who murdered to steal the possessions of passers by and also cannibalized the bodies of his victims.
- Madam de Brinvilliers, 17th Century French women who murdered family members in order to inherit their wealth.
- Catherine Montvoisin, another 17th Century French women who arranged for the elimination of hundreds of infants in return for payment.
- Baron Gilles de Rais from France. Who may be considered the true "father" of modern serial murderers.

The Baron was born into a family who possessed a great fortune, in the year 1404. He possibly murdered at least 800 children during an 8-year span. The magnitude and hideousness of his crimes was in complete opposition to his apparent

character.

As his biographer Leonard Wolf wrote, "as the children were dying, Gilles the artist of terror, the skilled Latinist who read St. Augustine; Gillies devoted companion of Jeanne d'Arc, squatted on the bellies of the children studying their anguished faces breathing their dying sighs." It was known that the Baron sodomized the victims before and after the murders.

Gilles acted out his internal fantasies of power and control. In his case, although he had a great deal of power and control in life, he needed more. He needed the actual power of life and death. He played out his internal fantasy. He played God. Baron Gilles wanted all authority, and even chastised the lowly estate of those who were acting as his judges. He only capitulated following threats of torture and excommunication. As we will see, he possessed many of the traits of the serial killers of modern America. One needs to have only talked to Gary Heidnik, or to have read some of his letters to see the remarkable similarities.

From 1970 continuing even today, there were more individual serial murders reported then in all the previous American history combined. It is becoming a rapidly increasing problem in America. The following, though admittedly incomplete, is a list of known serial murderers in modern day America.

1920's: Earl Nelson; Coral Program

1930's: Albert Fish

1940's: Jarvous Catoe, Howard Unruh, William Heirens

1950's: Charles Sharkucathes

1960's: Melven Reeves, Albert De Salvo, Michael Lee Herrington, Larry Cord Murders of Cincinnati (unsolved), Richard Spec, Dr. Ronald E. Clark, Antone Costa, James Brudas, Charles Witman

1970's: William Pierre, Edmond J. Cody, Benjamin Franklin Mills, Charles Schmid, Jr., Girard John Schaefer, Herbert Mullin, Edmond Eneil Kemper, Bruce Henderson Shreeves, Dean Corll, Elmer Wayne Henly, Julian Kennedy, Larry C. Creen, Joseph Calanger, "Zodiac Killers", Thomas E. Creech, Vaugh Greenwood, Dr. Mario E. Jascalevich, Patrick Kearny, Ennis Biarehi, Angelo Buno, Jr., Gary Jean Tison, Joseph Fischiz, John Gacy, Theodore Bundy, Gerald Eugene Staro, Juan Carina, David Berkowitz, Paul Knoules, Mark Essex, Vaugh Greenwood, Harvy Carignan, Edward Allavay.

1980 to 1984: Henry Lee Lucas, James Huberty, Author Bishof, Randal Woodfield, Gerald Starro, "The Green River Killer", Alton Coleman, Christopher Wilder, Robert Hanse, Michael Silka, Louis Hastings, Charles Meach, Robert Diez, Wayne Williams, "Trailside Slayings", Douglas Daniel Clark, Coral Eugene Watts, Randy Steve Kraft, Frederick Tyman Hodge, Larry Egler, William Benin, Joseph Christopher, Donald Miller, Steve Morin, Michael Ross, Michael Lewis Norris, Lawrence S. Bildtiber, "The Hitchhiker Slayings", Carlton Gary, "The Skid Row Slasher", "The Midtown Slasher", Coral Eugene Roberts, "The Atlanta-Georgia Thimon Murders", "The Houston-Texas Sunday Morning Slashings", David Bullock, Dale Robert Henderson, Joseph John Siellrin, William Benvior, Benard Durton Hunerick, Christine Falling, Henry Lee Lucas,

Otto Tool, Henry Brison, Richard Begerwald, Charles Hatcher, Douglas David Clark, Jeanine Jones, Geraldo Gallego, Debra Sue Tuggle, Joseph Paul Franklin, Robert Harson, Caulen Perry, Christopher Wilden, Robert R. Druz, Richard Rinarien.

(Source: Joel Norris, Elliot Leyton, Ann Rule.)

Obviously, the problem with serial murders in America is one in which the mental health profession must study, regardless of whether there was an actual increase over the centuries or not. The mere fact of the increasing number [there is no sound procedure for estimating the number of serial murderers at large in America today] of known serial murderers in the United States necessitates the development of more research and a diagnostic process must be completed if only for the public protection.

CHAPTER 2

THE DIAGNOSTIC CATEGORY OF SERIAL KILLER

CHARACTERISTICS OF A SERIAL KILLER

In June, 1988, in Philadelphia, Pennsylvania, during *The Commonwealth of Philadelphia v Gary M. Heidnik* trial, there was an opportunity to conduct thousands of hours of research in preparation for the trial. The research entailed a careful long-term interviewing process of Heidnik, as well as a comprehensive data and a review of the relevant scientific journals.

It was during the preparation of these data and after careful review and study that the patterns of a serial killer began to emerge. Specifically, it was apparent that Gary M. Heidnik posed these categories at various levels. It was also obvious, that evaluating Heidnik's sanity using The M'Naghten test had little to do with whether in fact, Heidnik was or was not insane. In evaluating a ritualistic serial killer with a compulsive personality a well trained psychologist or psychiatrist can find enough information to show that the individual was aware of the quality in nature of the act they were committing. This is because the rituals and compulsions of these individuals appear to in-

dicate logical thinking. These same professionals can then render an opinion that the individual was or was not insane. Often this opinion, as in the case of Gary Heidnik, is merely one more medical opinion of an individual that was seen by over 150 psychiatrists or psychologists during a 26 year period.

The compulsive ritual of a serial murderer has been rehearsed to perfection, with an overactive fantasy life, sometimes for decades. These rituals are rehearsed and improved further with each kidnapping or murder. A level of logical thinking and awareness is an inevitable conclusion.

After careful review of all the records, medical, legal, these data reveal that Gary M. Heidnik is insane, the jury's verdict not withstanding. That conclusion is based on factual evidence drawn from information that shows a 26 year period of mental illness and instability. Research by others has shown that someone who is apparently insane at the time of the commission of crime, probably had a similar history of insanity in the past. This is also the case with the serial murderers or ritualistic killers. There are numerous predictors which can be observed and attended to by professionals and lay people as well. The characteristics that serial or ritualistic murderers have in common become particularly clear when one studies the files of many of these killers. These observations show that some or all of the characteristics are present in these individuals.

One characteristic often noted, but seldom acted upon, is that these individuals often fall through the cracks of mental health in the criminal justice systems. *This is a result of the fact that there is no single diagnostic category that fits these individuals.* The pathology of serial murderer is a separate diagnostic category. It should be noted however, that the individual serial murderer may possess distinguishable psychiatric characteristics specific only to that individual which in no way diminishes the need for nor the recognition of this new diagnostic category.

As a group, serial killers do not pass the M'Naghten test

composed by the legal system. As a result, they are most often found legally sane. Thus far, research has shown that serial killers unanimously receive the death penalty, if they plead not guilty of insanity for their crimes.

Only Harrison Marty Graham, in Philadelphia, went through a trial and received a sentence of life in prison. Joel Moldovsky, Graham's attorney, carefully crafted his defense of Graham. In an interview with Joel Moldovsky, he explained that at the preliminary trial, the prosecution had such gruesome pictures and video tapes of the crimes, that a jury would never be able to hear the facts. He felt that the impact of these pictures and tapes on the emotions of twelve ordinary citizens would compel them to the death penalty. Mr. Moldovsky presented the evidence in such an artful and professional manner that the judge based the decision to spare Graham's life on this presentation and sentenced him to life in prison. The judges decision was made on the basis of Graham's mental illness, mental retardation, drug addiction and history of desperation virtually since birth. This was perhaps the only defense of a serial killer where the issue of insanity, and the diagnostic criteria of a serial murderer, were used to base the judicial decision (even if it was done so not knowing the specific category of a serial murderer).

Another common characteristic of serial murderers are there insatiable obsessions and almost instinctual drives that seemed to have pushed them to the ritualistic type of murder. In many cases these instinctual drives are exacerbated by complicated delusional thoughts and grandiose auditory and visual hallucinations. It is important to note that many researchers, including Joel Norris, in his book *Serial Killers*, described this obsession or need as a phase similar to the aura phase. This phase can also be described as a fantasy or deeply internal phase. Dr. Norris' conclusion is that this phase is often similar to the aura of a seizure victim. My research presents a different explanation of the etiology of the "aura" phase. The aura is often described as warmth flowing up through the

body and tingling sensations. Somewhere and at sometime during this phase, the individuals looses touch with reality. In addition this phase is often severely complicated in those individuals who may also have hallucinations. This phase is driven by an insatiable need to fill their empty lives.

In their study of thirty-six (36) men, convicted of sexual homicide, Ressler, Burgess, Douglas (1988), in looking for an antecedent and trigger to the first murder found that as a group, they were :

(1) aware of their long standing preoccupation and preference for a very active fantasy life, and

(2) devoted to violent, sexualized thoughts and fantasies. Most of these fantasies, prior to the first murder focused on killing. This contrasts with fantasies that evolved after the first murder; these advanced levels of fantasies often focused focused on perfecting various phases of the murder.

Additional research in the last few decades have supported these findings of Ressler, et.al. The major conclusion being that fantasy is a factor in sexual homicide. Several studies have suggested that sadistic sexual acts are associated with fantasy and that fantasy thought patterns were established early in life and existed in the context of social isolation. (Brittain, 1970; Reinhardt 1975; West, Roy and Nicholas, 1978)

Combined with the research into thinking patterns and research into sadistic fantasies (Brittain 1970); McCulloch, Snowdend, Wood and Mills in 1978 and Ressler in 1985 formulated the hypothesis that "the motivation for sexual murder is fantasy."

The fantasy is often the first area in the serial murderer's life in which he has control. The development of this fantasy is

a form of self-stimulating, self-reinforcing behavior that allows some self-control. It is often a sexual, masturbating behavior that is part of a larger fantasy.

The reinforcing value of the fantasy and the ability to get excitation and orgasm decreases as the fantasy is actually implemented. Therefore in order to increase these to the previous levels, the fantasy must be expanded or increased. The next reinforcing quality is the systematic increase in the sexual nature of the fantasy. This is often combined with masturbatory behavior as Ressler reported in 1988. Of the 36 serial murderers studied 81% admitted to compulsive masturbation.

As the individual fantasy looses its reinforcing quality, the internal thought process produces a more violent, sadistic fantasy. This increases the reinforcing quality of the behavior, which in turn increases the strength of the fantasy.

Thus everytime the fantasy is increased, its length grows, and the strength of the drive increases. It is a classic stimulus → response → stimulus → response in the form of reinforcement.

Once these fantasies have been extended to extreme sadistic lengths, the internal mechanism needed to increase the behavior may be exhausted. Therefore the overwhelming, uncontrollable drive to achieve reinforcement is to then move the internal fantasy to the external fantasy.

It is essential to realize that these fantasies are combined with autoeroticism. The reinforcing behavior is achieved by mental or sexual climax. When the fantasy is no longer effective at achieving orgasm the fantasy has to be increased.

Finally, the internal requires the external fantasy to be effective. Once the behavior becomes external and an actual murder takes place, that event is incorporated into the internal fantasy and masturbatory behavior. The actual murder and ritual behaviorism remain in the internal fantasy until they no

longer reference the fantasy to achieve orgasm.

Now, the internal needs require the external behaviors to provide reinforcement. The first murder has been expanded upon within the internal world by the fantasy. Therefore to reinforce the behavior in the external world, the fantasy adds new sadistic behaviors. Every behavior, external and internal, is maintained, increased or decreased by the strength of the antecedent and subsequent behavior. Thus behaviors are maintained by a continuing series of stimulus, response, stimulus reactions [S ➛ R ➛ S behavior].

The thought pattern employed by the serial killer in vivid with images of torture and ritual. These thoughts become more and more exciting to the killer. The thoughts and the thought patterns reinforce the behavior, until the ultimate reinforcement is actually acting out that behavior. *During the time when the behavior is acted out, what was the internal fantasy becomes an external reality that involves torture and death for a victim.*

It is important to realize that each act, or fantasy reinforces the previous action and thought-fantasy. Therefore the intensity of the murderer's behavior, once acted out, will continue until death or capture.

The child who started fires or was cruel to animals may move into thoughts of body mutilation. The only concern of the killer is to engage in acts which reinforce that is to murder and avoid capture or punishment.

The strength and reinforcing qualities of these thoughts and fantasies are stronger than the possible, potential punishment. As the fantasy continues to develop, the practice eliminates any potential negative consequences and increases the strength of the act. When the fantasy becomes an external reality the same S ➛ R ➛ S process takes place. The avoidance of punishment, of being caught becomes part of the fantasy reinforcement. The potential strength of this is overpowering. Gary Heidnik, would go to any length to avoid detection and

punishment. This was not a logical "real world" reaction, but part of the fantasy. It was what he had become.

In 1963, psychologist John McDonald suggested that three factors could predict violent behavior. Specifically, he suggested that a specific set of childhood behaviors were predictive of violent behavior in later life. These were bed wetting, fire starting, and the torture of small animals, better known as "McDonald's Triad." This was further developed by Hellman and Blackman who speculated that enuresis was actually a form of aggression directed against parental rejection.

G.S. Evseef and E.M. Wisniewski have also reported a theory of childhood experiences that suggest "homicidal proneness." While these early studies are all relevant, there are additional criteria.

If one looks at the studies of juveniles who later murdered, there are five (5) characteristics that appear consistently. These are:

- major neurological impairment;
- psychotic symptoms;
- psychotic disorders among first degree relatives;
- physical or sexual abuse;
- severe violence or destruction as a juvenile.

(Lewis, May, Jackson, Aaronsen, Restito, Serra and Simos, 1985.)

Ressler, Douglas and Burgess (1988) analyzed the behavior of potential serial murderers and added the following information:

1. As a group, serial murderers were aware of their long standing preoccupation and preference for a very active fantasy life;

2. Devoted to violent, sexualized thoughts and fantasies, most of the fantasies, prior to the first murder, focused on killing.

In addition, within these five characteristics, there are three classes which have been noted. One is the individual who has deep religious experiences. This may be complicated by visions, feeling of grandiosity, and sessions of speaking to a deity such as Jesus Christ, or god. It is often during this phase when the individuals are told by their "deity" to perform certain acts on their victims. Another complication of this phase includes visual or auditory hallucinations, and having a mother or other authority figure directing the individual to perform certain acts. It can also be seen to be very similar to a (seizure-like) phase where the individual is driven by other characters within their own personalty. The research shows that many of these individuals are driven by fantasy latent, hypersexual desire. This feeling has been described as similar, but by no means identical to an individual who is abusing amphetamines. In the case of Harrison Marty Graham, these feelings were further complicated by his usage of Ritalin and Talwin injections. It would seem then that this aura phase could be precipitated by the use of drugs, either street or prescription.

Gary Heidnik, the prime subject of this research, never used street drugs. It is significant however that from 1962 right through to the present, he has been on major psychiatropic medication including Thorazine, and Stelazine.

These phases are often misinterpreted as the individual serial killers attempt to malinger or to pretend that they are a multiple personality. As Ressler has pointed out, many serial killers are able to pass polygraph tests. Although these test may work for normal people, psychopaths have been know to possess the ability to separate the personality that commits the

crime from the other self. People such as Gary Heidnik, can separate such components of his personality. Bishop Gary, G.M. Kill, and Gary Heidnik were all one person, yet they all operated separately within his personality. Another part of this aura is often the feeling as if someone was taking over the individual. In the case of John Wayne Gacy, he had a specific person who he identified but he also was seen as a manipulator.

Serial killers are manipulative, this characteristic does not come under the category of multiple personality. Aware of the different personalities within them often the serial killer feels as if he has been directed by one of these personalities and has no ability to stop. It one looks at this as a cross between an instinctual drive and a aura phase it can be said that these individuals are in the process of having a seizure-like behavior. Psychomotor type seizure behavior has been reported by numerous researchers doing investigations into the serial killer phenomenon.

Many serial killers often have strong feelings of inadequacy. These feeling maybe masked by numerous artificial successes, but the feelings run deeper than the normal neurotic feeling of not being good enough. In the case of Gary Heidnik who had scored as high as 148 in intelligent testing, has substantial financial portfolio, and was a bishop in his own church feelings of inadequacy were still strong. John Wayne Gacy in Chicago ran a successful business, was involved in politics, and organized a parade with Rosilyn Carter, he also had distinct feeling of inadequacy.

In the case of Gary Heidnik specifically the feelings of inadequacy were such that his thinking was often confused because of his low self-esteem. When given a Minnesota multiphasic inventory (MMPI), he was observed to have an extremely high schizophrenic score (126). It was noted that individuals having this profile are generally characterized as having feeling of inadequacy, hostility, poor judgment, and inability to concentrate along with confused or delusional thinking.

This finding was later confirmed in several tests that Heidnik was given throughout his career.

The feelings of inadequacy often belie the external apparent successful nature of the personality. Joel Norris labeled this a "mask of sanity." All the serial killers that I have investigated have this mask of sanity. In addition they have all also portrayed themselves as their victims in one way or another.

It was found in both the Heidnik and Graham investigations that throughout their lives, neither was ready to accept responsibility for determining his past experiences. To this day, Gary Heidnik feels that he is a victim of sensationalism surrounding his trial. Although this maybe partly true, it is quite clear that the heinous nature of the crimes beget sensational publicity. The other serial killers such as Gacy always portrayed himself as the victim of systems, parents, schools, governments but never himself.

One other characteristic of serial killers is that they all attempt to get help. They appear to want to stop what is about to happen yet they always regain control of themselves to prevent their discovery.

With Heidnik in particular there were volumes of data predicting the tragedy which would come in his future. Heidnik had been sentenced in 1978 for kidnapping the sister of his common law wife from a mental retardation facility in Pennsylvania. When his kidnaped victim was found it was in a locked closet in the basement near Gary Heidnik's apartment. During one phase of his life, while in Fairview State Hospital for the Criminally Insane, Heidnik remained mute for three years because "the devil put a cookie in this throat." During a Parole Board hearing, he remained mute and only passed notes. He went into that meeting with a Bible, the pages of which were highlighted "though the passages were Satan remove voices and biblical characters became mute. His muteness remained until one day he entered a church and during the services his voice returned. In these Parole Board hearings, which took

place over a series of months, Heidnik sighed his name to the Parole Board request as G. M. Kill instead of Gary M. Heidnik. Heidnik wanted to stay in the hospital; he knew he needed help.

In a November 1992 *Frontline* interview on PBS television, convicted child molester and serial killer John Wesley Dodd points out how the murders he committed could have been prevented:

> "...I don't know. I can't really say I've discovered much about myself. I think really the biggest thing is that everything could have been prevented. I've gotten...I've had so many contacts with police and confessed to so many crimes and never been charged, or the charges were dropped and I was never prosecuted for one reason or another. ... I first started exposing myself when I was 13 years old. My first contact with the police came when I was 15. On March 10 of 1977, I was arrested by the Richland Police Department here in Washington and confessed to six or seven crimes. I don't remember for sure...these seven cases probably involved close to 20 kids."

Dodd was released by a judge for two reasons. Only part of his record was available for review during the trial and sentencing, and Dodd made a "good appearance" in court and appeared to be a normal, reasonable person.

This quest for help can be found in the records of almost every serial killer investigated. It became especially clear in the Heidnik case because his records are relatively complete and thorough. Heidnik's subsequent behavior had been predicted many times. For example, when interviewed by a psychiatrist in 1984 Heidnik was found to have persecutory grandiose delusions, disoriented insight, and judgment severely impaired.

He was found to be incompetent. This same psychiatrist predicted heinous crimes would be committed by Heidnik in the future, or he would hurt himself.

Another characteristic that is common among serial killers is an internal battle that they struggle with between intimacy and control. At times, it appears that this battle for control is one that is life long. They are often raised in a home where there is no closeness or intimacy. The result is that the only way that they know how to relate to others is through the abusive behavior the parent taught them as a child.

It can easily be seen that their feelings of inadequacy come from the severe rejection of their parents. This emotional rejection usually takes the form of emasculation. This abuse can be so severe and so constant that the abuse itself becomes the model for how they will control their own life. It becomes the only form of closeness through contact that they know. Later in life when they attempt to form relationships they have no ability to interrelate. They have no capacity to experience intimacy. These people never feel the closeness or intimacy of bonding even with their own parents when they were children. Their relationships come through only control and their ability or inability to be in control.

Their feelings of inadequacy are such that even if their masculinity has them appear as if they are in control of themselves on the outside, internally they are in torment and constant severe pain. If they are in a relationship it often fails. They are abusive because they can not control through any other means. The people they victimize are people that have characteristics that they have found a way to control. The control is sometimes through force, some of the victims have a low subnormal IQ, appear naive or may have been given drugs or alcohol to make them cooperate. Often the act of murder comes in the form of ultimate control. Gacy would strangle people producing a sexually free final act of control. Many other serial killers strangulation or torture produced the same

results, a high and a release of pain and a sexual climax. These are people who can not control themselves and can not control a relationship, who are not able to be intimate because they have never experienced it. (For a detailed explanation of intimacy and control communications read *The Intimacy Manual* by Amidon, Amidon, Apsche, Stivers & Silverman. International Information Associates Inc., 1992).

When closeness or intimacy is denied by a parent, the child continues to seek intimacy or closeness. When control is substituted for intimacy, the child seeks the reinforcement through internalized thoughts that later grow to fantasies.

If the child is consistently punished, rather than reinforced by the parents, two behaviors are learned:

- ☐ Control is more powerful than intimacy;
- ☐ Punishment is more powerful than reinforcement.

(See Axelrod and Apsche [Eds], *Punishment and Its Effects on Human Behavior* for a complete review of this topic.)

Therefore, the mold if formed, and the result is a person who will use power and control in his/her interpersonal relationships. Also important in this early development is the fact that the only control the child has is over their own internal thoughts and fantasies.

One of the areas that prosecuting attorneys in serial murder trials develop to a great extent is the concept of malingering. Both Harrison Marty Graham and Gary M. Heidnik were accused by their prosecutors of being malingerers. They were allegedly malingering to collect social security funds or veterans benefits. In the case of Gary Heidnik the prosecution claimed that he was hospitalized so frequently in order that he would maintain his veterans benefits under title 38 of the U.S. code. It could be found that Heidnik qualified retroactively for his benefits and did not need hospitalization to maintain these benefits. Therefore, if an individual is hospitalized, re-

quests to remain hospitalized, because he or she is afraid of their own fantasies knows that they will murder are they malingering? The Heidnik case in particular there were 13 documented suicide attempts with the prosecuting attorney dismissing these as malingering because none were successful.

Suicide is a characteristic allied to the feelings of inadequacy that is found in many serial killers. In one of the 13 suicide attempts Heidnik was found comatose and was intubated and in need of respiratory support, he was injected Narcan, he contracted pneumonia during the subsequent hospitalization. This was rejected by the legal system as malingering because the attempt was unsuccessful and Heidnik lived.

It is important to remember that serial killers as a group develop their own set of reality. However the extensive research work "Heidnik Reality" could be specified. If as Heidnik you are functioning within a reality brought forth by a grandiose delusion or complex hallucination from god, or operating from other individuals or other authority figures in a hallucinatory or dry phase, you are a individual operating within your own reality. Heidnik was following god's plan. The initiation of his church, his church articles, even the inception of the church were all based on delusional and hallucinatory thinking.

In interviews with myself and the defense psychiatrist Kenneth Kool M.D. Heidnik stated that his ability to manipulate money such as growing $15,000 into $600,000, was due to his stock tips from god. He would not discuss the specifics of what god told him because of his pact with god. This is a clear delusional system.

The specifics of such systems are so private as between Heidnik and god that to divulge them would be an infringement on the pact with god. Therefore, his pact with god is more valuable then his own life. In documenting the Heidnik reality I observed 217 specific instances over the course of 22 hospitalizations that demonstrated Heidnik's inability to distin-

guish right from wrong and his impaired sense of judgment and reality. He clearly demonstrated the pattern of an emerging serial ritualistic killer.

According to A. Charles Peruto Jr., Heidnik's defense attorney, Heidnik's sense of reality was impaired enough for the jurors to have returned an initial poll of 10 for insanity and only 2 against. It was only after the instructions on the legal insanity defense that this jury think otherwise. The Heidnik trial gives evidence that the category of ritualistic serial murderers remains outside the real of expertise of the mental health professional, as well as the forensic psychiatrist. Serial killer is not in the traditional psychiatric or sociopathic diagnostic categories. The case of *The Commonwealth of Pennsylvania vs. Gary M. Heidnik* documents this fact.

Heidnik wanted children and followed gods plan to let him have those children. He kept women in his basement, all of them to be impregnated and to have children Indian style, that is naturally, so he could keep them. Lisa Thomas stated in an interview that Gary wanted 10 women, he wanted all 10 pregnant and all 10 to deliver naturally. He told them he could get them so drunk they would not feel the pain but he would not be able to stop the bleeding.

In fact, he wasn't interested in the women at all, only the children. Consider the fact that he would deny them any prenatal care or proper nutrition. They were made to live like animals in a hole in his basement all for the sole purpose of producing children for god-his god. This was his world not our world, not anyone else's world. This was the Heidnik reality as uncovered through interviews with Heidnik and with his victims.

In a comment during his court testimony, Gary Heidnik saw nothing wrong with, nor does he recognize anything he did as was wrong in that basement in Philadelphia. He did not intend to murder anyone himself but he wanted to follow gods plan. He did not want to be caught, he did not want to

lose his children. This paranoid delusional system remains totally intact today. He saw the women in his basement as the only means to his end. He saw them only as females who would produce his children. At his trial, he leaned over and asked his attorney A. Charles Peruto Jr., in my presence if they were still pregnant and he could not understand why they would still be mad at him. He merely wanted to have children. The Heidnik reality was in full bloom and he felt was that god told him to have children. God gave him instructions and Heidnik developed a plan and followed it. In his mind he had to adhere to gods law not man's therefore he did nothing wrong and god made his law apparent to Gary Heidnik. He maintains that he did not want to harm anyone.

If Heidnik was to have children as god told him, he could not let the women go, he could not get caught. He put them in the basement, turned up the volume of the radio to hide the sounds and moans of torture, and he followed gods plans. He punctured their ear drums with screw drivers to prevent them from hearing him enter or depart. Does any of that sound logical, malingering, sane, or insane? If people heard anyone scream and the police came, he would get caught and he would not have the children according to the plan of god. Remember Heidnik wanted to please god not man. It was not meant that he be discovered it was only meant that he had children.

According to Gary Heidnik he had talked to god for years. He began in the mid 1970's and he degenerated at a rapid pace form 1978 to the present. While in the armed services he experienced seizure-like behaviors that at the time were thought to be hallucinatory and delusional. He had conversations with god, and Jesus came to him in bright lights and made him feel warm and tingly all over. It seemed clear that his sense of reality was not that of societies but was that of gods. Keep in mind that this is a complex sense based on delusional hallucinatory system that is possibly produced by his fantasy driven behavior. The need to move his internal fantasy to the

external world became the behavior. These produced the "hallucinating effect," or an active delusion.

Heidnik lost 4 children through the court systems and because of his abuse to his wife and common law wife, he would not let that happen again. He would listen to god this time. He knew it was god, he was sure. It was only the rest of us in society that could determine that he was not talking to god and that he was wrong.

Over his life time Heidnik made 13 suicide attempts. He was evaluated by 150 psychiatrists and hundreds of mental health professionals. Many of these professionals warned of what would come in the future. Gary Heidnik himself signed his name G.M. Kill. He predicted his future behavior in a series of letters to the Parole Board and to his psychiatrist. Based on the study of Army records, hospital and prison records Gary Heidnik spent more time in treatment at psychiatric hospitals then he spent out of treatment. Heidnik may have been delusional for most of his life. From 1962 on he operated purely within his delusional system of god.

As was mentioned Heidnik was mute for more than 1,005 days from 1978 until 1981, because the devil put a cookie in his throat. Heidnik told the author and A. Charles Puerto Jr. that he was surprised that the Parole Board did not see the cookie in his throat. He felt that at that point he was not following god's plan and he was therefore being punished.

Heidnik started his church in 1970 after driving his 1964 Plymouth to Malibu for coffee and donuts. He left his apartment hungry for coffee and donuts and kept driving excessively across the country as if possessed. During this time he was definitely in a aura phase or delusional phase and he met god in Malibu, California. God told him to go back to Philadelphia and start a church where he was to be bishop. He again followed god's plan and became Bishop Gary Heidnik. His church had a constitution and was founded the way many other churches are following gods law, not man's. From this it

can be seen that Gary Heidnik should have had one hospitalization not 22. *He was clearly insane, the insanity displayed is that a new category — serial killer.*

Serial killers are a product, as a group of homes with little or no closeness. In a study of males born in the Philadelphia area in 1945 Marvin Wolfgang demonstrated how children of abusive homes became abusive themselves. In his book *Serial Killers* Dr. Joel Norris lists abuse physical or emotional, as a characteristic for serial killers. There are individuals who are brought into this world as unwanted baggage. Parents are cruel or abrasive alcoholics or drug addicts.

According to A. Charles Puerto Jr. it was disclosed in an interview with Heidnik's brother that Gary had been hung outside a third floor window by his feet for disobeying is father at the age of 3. The reason was that he did not clean his room to his fathers satisfaction. His mother was married five times and was an alcoholic. Other serial killers have similar backgrounds. Harrison Marty Graham was shifted back and forth to a foster home. He has a pronounced scar on his head from a beating by his mother. He was admitted to a hospital with a concussion and a wide open contusion needing sutures. Joseph Kallinger was told by his foster parents that he would have his penis removed if he had an erection. John Wayne Gacy's father was an alcoholic, abusive and constantly belittling him. Gacy's mother told him that his father had a brain tumor and Gacy had to behave so as not to upset his father or his tumor would explode. His father was an abusive perfectionist and Gacy was never good enough.

The need in all human beings for bonding should be apparent. Harrlows' Reces monkey experiment demonstrated that this is an instinctual need. When a human being does not bond in infant stages, it appears that their basic need to be close remains unfulfilled. Later in life, the need becomes a life long need or an obsession. The office of therapists are crowded with a wide variety of neurotics expressing exactly

that need.

When control is substituted for intimacy, such as in the case of abuse by a mentally ill father and an alcoholic mother, the child mistakenly assumes that control and/or manipulation are substitutes for intimacy, closeness and belonging. Even in non-psychotic populations there is a conflict of intimacy and control. Dr. Edmund Amidon has shown that people often confuse issues with regard to intimacy and control. He has shown that normal individuals substitute control when intimacy needs are uncontrollable or unmet.

Dr. Richard G. Rappaport, a forensic psychiatrist, writes that the sexual sadist is in need of taking or demonstrating his power. He sees that the actual murder itself becomes a form of intimacy between the killer and the victim. "The mode of death is one where factors indicate that the victim has meaning for the killer and that the intimacy in the murderous act is part of a close bond between himself and the victim formed in the killers fantasy and delusions." The killer actually substitutes control for intimacy. The killer has never felt intimacy in his or her life. Control, through abuse, both emotional and physical, has been substituted for intimacy. In their book *Mass Murder: America's Growing Menace,* Jack Levine and James Fox talk about control in serial killers when they state that the pleasure and exhilaration that serial killers derive from repeated murders stems from the absolute control they have over human being. As Roy Norris admitted about his assaults against women, "the rape wasn't really the important part, it was the dominance." In many cases such as that of Ted Bundy this form of control is the only way they can achieve orgasm.

If control was substituted throughout life for intimacy the sex and sexual gratification are a form of control not intimacy. Ressler et. al. talk about their interviews with thirty-six serial killers. They show how the killers internal world is filled with troublesome and emotionless thoughts of dominance [control] over others. Their entire lives are built on control. Con-

trol has been substituted for intimacy or bonding. The actual act of torture and murder has been reported by these men as POWER. For them POWER = CONTROL.

The extent of the control necessary may have a inverse relationship with the amount of abuse they were exposed to as children. As an example of this, "the girl in the box" of Red Bluff, California. In her book *Perfect Victim*, Christine McGuire, the prosecuting attorney, detailed the abusive sado-masochistic sex perpetrated by Cameron Hooker upon Colleen Stand, his captive and sex slave for seven years. Both in the book and in person Christine McGuire maintains that Hooker was a product of a non-physical abusive childhood.

Upon careful examination of the details in the book, it is apparent that Hooker was a product of an emotionally abusive household. The statement can be made by assessing the fact that his father once walked in on a wiping of Colleen by Hooker and supposedly did not see it.

In addition they had to be aware of the abnormal relationship between Cameron and his wife. I do believe that there was little or no physical abuse in his childhood, yet there was a great deal of abnormality of emotion. Thus, in support of the supposition that the need to control is based on a combination of physical and emotional abuse, Hooker did not murder, he only abused her. His insatiable need stopped short of murder.

As a child, Cameron Hooker may have been a product of an abnormal environment what he dealt to Colleen Stand was, physical and emotional abuse, but not death. Where sexual killers are products of physical, emotional, and often sexual abuse, they may in turn murder.

The serial killer never experienced normal bonding or intimacy therefore control and power over their victims was substituted for intimacy. This need for intimacy is eventually released in the form of total control that is the actual death of

the victim. As Dr. Rappaport suggests, the actual mode of death is one more factor for the killers reality between intimacy and control. In cases where there are necrophilia and cannibalism are an extension of the ultimate control or possession to a point after death. In this manner the control can continue long after the "murderous organisms."

Harrison Marty Graham possessed seven bodies because of this insatiable need for control. He kept the bodies to fulfill his sadistic sexual pleasures. He kept these bodies until parts of them actually rotted off.

Gary Heidnik kept his hostages in a basement dungeon. According to Lisa Thomas, Heidnik eventually feed her and other victims parts of the body of Sandra Lindsey. The flesh cooked and mixed with dog food and rice. The remainder of the body parts were stored in the freezer. This is the ultimate in control and possession. To feed the body parts of a former hostage to the remaining hostages. In that way they remain captive in the digestive tract of other slaves, totally controlled.

There is at this time no cure for serial murderers. In treatment they will revert to their helpful, eager to please, manipulative and affable selves. They are uncontrollably sadistic, barring treatment break through will never be cured. At the same time they are not in control of or responsible for their actions. It should be kept in mind that whenever these people are paroled they will murder again. Kemper, Gacy, Bundy, Yuki, Kellinger, and Heidnik and all others prove this beyond a shadow of a doubt. These people should be placed in secure mental facilities to be studied and hopefully understood. This would allow us to minimize the threat of the serial murderer to the public safety and health.

The remaining chapters of the book appear in greater detail the findings which lead to the stated conclusions. It should be noted that this work represents only the first steps in the establishment of serial killer diagnostic category and in the treatment and understanding of the serial killer. This new diagnos-

tic category must be avidly researched and reviewed by the psychiatric and psychological community. Extensive research needs to be completed on the diagnostic criterion for serial killers in order to prevent these tragedies in the future.

CHAPTER 3

FANTASY: THE BEGINNING

During a personal interview, Gary Heidnik said: " ... fantasy is better than reality, nothing can go wrong, it's the way you want it." According to Ressler and Shachtman in their book, *Whoever Fights Monsters,* all the serial killers that Ressler interviewed during his twenty year career in the FBI had fantasies. All the murderers that we interviewed had compelling fantasies; they murdered to make happen in the real world, what they had seen over and over in their minds since childhood and adolescence.

In further discussions, correspondence and other contacts with Gary Heidnik, it was apparent that he has always attempted to portray himself as the victim. He was always the underdog. Gary Heidnik was the pitiful character that had never had a break. He had obviously, and accurately, perceived my blind spot for victims, and my visual compassion for the underprivileged. At times I believed him. I felt sorry for him. But through research, more interviews, and my own self-directed anger at being manipulated, I have come to know Heidnik. I have been able to exact "the truths" from his diatribes and his pedantic intellectualism. In a later section of this book on Motive, I will develop a practical and theoretical explanation of his fantasy, his internal world and its working and intricacies.

This chapter will develop from beginning to end, Heidnik's fantasy life. This will be accomplished by using Heidnik's own words along with my own interpretations. These "truths" were shifted from reams of letters and documents written by, and about Gary M. Heidnik.

THE BEGINNINGS IN HEIDNIK'S WORDS

It is easy to see the beginnings of a life of fantasy in these words from a letter written by Gary Heidnik while in prison after his conviction:

> As I mentioned previously I have managed to overcome the perception of being retarded as a child. I have flunked second grade once and was about to flunk again when dad worked with me and made me learn. Even better he started a fire in me where by I liked to read books. (That reading) became a problem since it warped my sense of reality. I couldn't see things as they really were I saw them vicariously through the eyes of people like Edgar Rice Burroughs.

Several questions about Heidnik's early years became apparent after studying this particular passage.

- ☐ Why did other kids see him as being retarded?
- ☐ Did Dad really help him, and if so how?
- ☐ Did the reading warp his sense of reality or did it fill the void in an already internal process?

After comparing that passage with transcripts from his trials and interviews with Heidnik's family members it revealed it-

self as the beginnings of a "loner" an outcast. According to Terry Heidnik the kids always made fun of Gary. They called him football head. Apparently young Gary Heidnik had a odd shaped head and looked ridiculous. It also appears that Gary would often preferred to spend time alone rather than with others. Thus his reading gave him an excuse to be alone in his fantasy world. Reading then helped to fill a void, actually it became an unknowing fuel for his fantasy life.

Did Gary Heidnik's father really help him? By both Heidnik's' brothers description dad was a stern disciplinarian. Terry described out-right abuse by the father. "He actually hit Gary on the head with a board and hung him out of his 3rd floor bedroom window by his feet." Gary only states that dad was a stern disciplinarian or an "Archie Bunker" type. But Gary Heidnik would not say anything derogatory about either his father or his mother. If you were to listen to his descriptions of his home life it's as if he grew up with Ward and June Cleaver. It is apparent that this is an outright manipulation, his attempt to give little to help piece together the puzzle. "I'm not very bright," Gary Heidnik December 26, 1988. [148 —very superior intelligence —March 16, 1987.]

In reference to Heidnik in her March 16, 1987 report, court psychologist Eva Wojclechowski states: "Heidnik currently tests within very superior limits of the range of intelligence. He assimilates novel material quickly and has an accumulated an above average level of academic information. This man is extremely alert to environmental details and he has above average comprehension and judgment."

The preceding paragraph has been inserted simply to inject some reality into the fantasy world of Gary Heidnik. It is extremely important to be grounded in facts whenever dealing with Gary Heidnik. He has the ability to make many situations seem believable and feasible. It is difficult not to believe what he says. He is capable of giving an extremely convincing argument to prove that he is not bright and that he is slow and

possibly even mentally retarded. But back to Gary Heidnik's fantasy world in his own words.

> I use to think that when I was about 14 or 15 that I could live in the woods, hunt with a knife, and a riffle and surge through the trees. Really! I actually thought I could swing through the trees like Tarzan and run away from home to do so. Fortunately, I took one look at the trees and came to my senses before I actually tried.

> The biggest way books and lack of social life warped my thinking is in regards to interpersonal relationships. *I couldn't see or relate to people as they really are.* [Italics are the authors] I always perceived them vicariously through the eyes of fiction writers. People aren't like the ones in the fictional stories, especially in the books available in the 50s.

Attempting to manufacture sympathy and understanding Heidnik talked a bit of the safe parts of his internal world. The fact that he realized that he could not relate to people as they are in the external world and could only relate to people internally is one example. Whenever Gary attempted to fit those in his external world to those in his internal world it would leave him frustrated, angry and retreating back into his own mind to a world that he created in it. Heidnik continues:

> I'm good in vocabulary though which boosts my IQ score but vocabulary is largely memorizing. With my love of reading they reinforce each other. But I'm slow! As they say in the vernacular, I'm slow on my feet. It just took two weeks to read 300 pages of the *Iliad*. I've done well educationally by not over loading myself. Since I am so slow

mentally, I can only devote so much time to the most important matters. In schools for instance, I had no social life. No parties, friends, girls, zip! I used that time to study and get good grades and please my father.

Yes, it was important for Gary to please his father, for if he did not please him he would face his wrath.

It takes a lot of effort on my part to achieve the educational levels I have made. But I do it with a little extra effort and an analytical mind. When something puzzles me or if I have a problem I will spend hours on it trying to solve it in an analytical fashion. I can play a tremendous game of chess but it takes me so long that it drives the other players crazy. I'll study each and every move until I've analyzed most possibilities and then make my move. Taking hours and hours to play a game.

Gary Heidnik develops his credo as a code. He does not miss any move. He is extremely bright, aware and analytical. In his own words Heidnik discounts all his previous statements about him not being bright or a poor snook. Remember intelligence is based on abstract analysis as well as on an ability to solve problems. It is most important to be aware that Heidnik related that he premeditates every move. Therefore that it is obvious that he consciously aware and planned the entire crime street in his basement on Marshall Street in Philadelphia. He was aware and carefully planned his moves.

Heidnik rehearsed his fantasies until he was ready to incorporate them into his external world. He stated the central issue of the operation of his fantasy. "Like when I can play a tremendous game of chess but it takes me so long it drives the other players crazy." In this analogy Heidnik was referring to how he lives his life. How he plans his strategies. But it is key to

his fantasy. Just like chess plans, he analyzes and rehearses each move until he is sure that it will work. No surprises, no failures, but only in his fantasy.

> When I took that course on Child Sociology in the 60's at the University of Pennsylvania it was a big help in getting to understand why I was so screwed up. What it didn't explain was why people always hate me so much. I have no friends except the fellow disabled at 40th street.

Here is the crux of Gary's inability to bridge his internal world to his external world. He was only really in control in the internal fantasy. Externally it was never the way it was suppose to be.

> Who are the only people who would socialize with me? I like people. I also want to be liked! I don't like being lonely, but I can't seem to *master [Italics are Authors] interpersonal relationships,* and the harder I try the worse it gets. People use this desire of mine to be liked to their advantage and abuse me.

> They'd take advantage of me. The hardest thing I had to adjust to is giving up on people. If I say to myself my own affairs like in solitaire and in books I manage to stay out of conflicts. But if I try to socialize I wind up with problems. Sometimes big ones.

Here Heidnik actually explained his own inability to relate to the external world. He desires closeness and intimacy yet he has no means of achieving it. He attempts to "master" or control relationships since an early age he was conditioned to sub-

stitute control for intimacy. Since he can not feel intimacy he replaces it with anger and control. He justifies this through making himself the persecuted victim.

> If it wasn't for Tony I wouldn't have had anyone at my wedding. I didn't have a reception since who would come? Even my friend Jack Cassidy wouldn't come. Persecution is my middle name. People not only dislike me they like to persecute me. Just look at the records. It's bad enough not being liked but why do they persecute me when I've done nothing to them?

In contrast to those words are the comments in the report of court psychologist Eva Wojciechowski:

> Mr. Heidnik is highly suspicious, grandiose and at times delusional since Mr. Heidnik states that he is repeatedly contemplated suicide. He impressed this examiner as far more dangerous to others than to himself. Mr. Heidnik sees himself imbued with religious fervor and zeal: he mentioned several times to this examiner how he would avenge himself on those who crossed him...Mr. Heidnik is quite dangerous as his thinking is often times coldly logical and practical.

The court psychologist was right. Listen to these words of Gary Heidnik's from November 19, 1988.

> A unique way of looking what I did in my disturbed state of mind was to create my own social group. It was a social group in which I was the only male, the only economic provider, the patriarch so to speak and which was available to me 24 hours a day. Since I couldn't achieve a sense

of belonging to any other existing social groups in American society, I endeavored to create my own social group. One that had to accept me and couldn't abandon me and had to provide the things that I needed, love, bonding, children, companionship, etc.

For instance, anytime I felt a need to talk they were there. Where could they go? And they had to listen."

There it was Gary Heidnik's fantasy in full bloom. Bishop Gary the patriarch in control. He was actually able to cross from his internal delusional world to the external world. He created his fantasy in the basement of 3520 Marshall Street, Philadelphia, Pennsylvania. It worked for a time. It worked until it was discovered that Bishop Gary's heaven was a hell for the women.

CHAPTER 4

KIDNAPPING & RAPE: A WARNING

In 1978 Municipal Court Gary Heidnik was found not guilty of the kidnapping and rape of Alberta Davidson, who was the institutionalized retarded sister of his common law wife Angeanette. He was found guilty of wrongful imprisonment, and sentenced to 5 years at Graterford State Prison in Pennsylvania. *These events took place ten years before Heidnik kept his sexual slaves in a basement in Philadelphia.*

On May 7, 1978 Heidnik and Angeanette drove from Philadelphia to Sealingsgrove Center in Pennsylvania. Sealingsgrove is a state run institution for the mentally retarded in Central Pennsylvania, geographically not far from Penn State University in Happy Valley. But the geography and the surrounding beauty is where any comparison ends with regards to Sealingsgrove Center and Happy Valley. In 1978, the facilities were old, smelled of urine, and the staff was often indistinguishable from the clients. In fact, the old saying about institutions was appropriate to Sealingsgrove ... the only way you can tell the staff from the inmates is that the staff carries keys.

Alberta Davidson was institutionalized in Sealingsgrove. Heidnik and Angeanette signed her out for a weekend. They

never signed her back in.

On May 17th the staff social worker, Mrs. Snauffer and staff psychologist Dr. Bingham went to Heidnik's West Philadelphia house accompanied by the Philadelphia police and armed with a search warrant. Initially they feared nothing. Finally the psychologist opened the door to the apartment and called Alberta's name. They heard a faint but muffled reply some where in the basement. Alberta Davidson was found in an unlit storage closet in the basement, an old coal bin. This event had turned out to be prophetic. To be replayed with unimaginable horror years later at 3520 Marshall Street.

In questioning Heidnik regarding this event, it is best to have him explain it himself. The words are an excerpt from a letter addressed to myself dated January 31, 1988.

> Here are the details on the coal bin issue, which really nobody ever asked me about. You are the first who has ever been interested, to ever wonder about it. That morning I came home from work with Alberta and I found out later that Denise told them that she would come home with me. By the way, a day or two earlier at Family Court, these nice people from Sealingsgrove while my car was parked on Vine Street glued my car doors shut with super glue. They squatted super glue into the door lock so I couldn't get my key into the lock. Fortunately, they ran out of glue (or forgot) that the trunk and I got a screw driver out and was able to force an opening into the lock on the passenger side so we could get in and move the car. It was especially urgent to get in since we were in a rush. So in the morning they "persuaded" and they asked Alberta to return, I had come home and gone to bed. Alberta and

Angeanette were in the living room watching T.V. (I guess). I think but I am not sure that Snauffer started pounding on the door (the one I've marked). I ignored her. Then the phone rang and she told me she wanted to search my apartment since she knew that I had Alberta there. I agreed to let her in. I took Alberta out of the apartment immediately and hid her in the coal bin. The door to the bin was unlocked. Nobody disputes that, now look at the drawing I've enclosed, where it says heavy fire door.

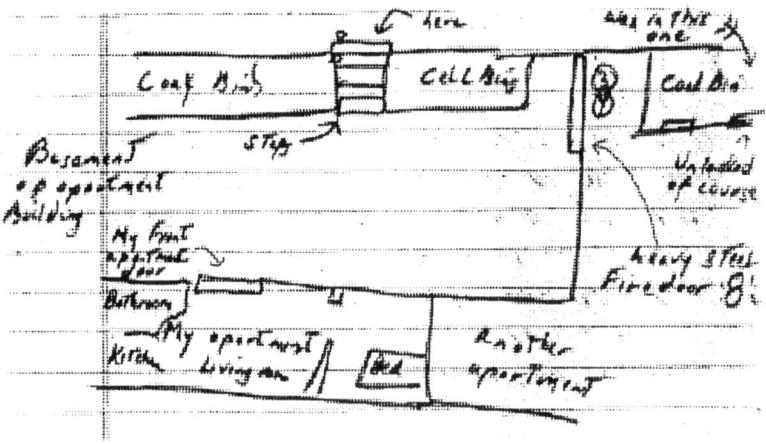

For some reason I thought that would lock and once closed and locked could only be opened from one side. (The one Alberta was on.) I told her to stay hidden there until I called and told her it was alright to come out and for her to then open the heavy door from her side since I didn't realize it could be opened from my side. (Foolish me.) She said she understood and would stay hidden until I called. We both really didn't think that Snauffer and her people could get through the fire door, but I hid her anyways. I had locked

the door to the coal bin, and she couldn't have gotten out to unlock the fire door right? Although there were a few problems here, as I said at the time I was in a big hurry to open the door for Snauffer. She claimed in court that she called me from a house across the street. A LIE. (But for what I don't know. Maybe to protect Audry Davis.) She called me from her apartment she had to since when Alberta and I passed her from my apartment to the coal bin she saw us.

She was also looking through the crack under the door. She didn't get a good look but enough to know we went that way! I knew she saw us because she told us that very day. To have seen us from under the door she'd have had to have made a call from Audry's apartment not the college student's across the street. She didn't have time to travel that far and back. But why did she LIE? Again I don't know. Anyways when I opened the door and let her in I got two surprises. The first was that she had a policemen with her and second that she never even went towards my apartment within the direction we had hidden Alberta. Then I got a third shock. An even bigger one then the first two the fire door opened right up. Then she went into the other hallway and called Alberta's name a couple of times.

Alberta messed up, probably was confused since she was suppose to be listening for me to call and answered Snauffer. I've already explained in the other letter how Snauffer persuaded Alberta to go back with them, I was not asked and I was so

slow on my feet. It never even occurred to me to tell Alberta she didn't have to go back. She could stay with us. Also about the putative rape of Alberta if I'm not mistaken the devious Snauffer never told the lie that Alberta said I raped her. I'm pretty sure that the lie never even came up and Snauffer never claimed she said I did anything. That kind of surprises me why a gifted liar like Snauffer wouldn't at least claim Alberta said this. And apparently they were already back to Sealingsgrove before they started to lay plans to frame me. I wasn't there so I don't know what they did, so I suppose they had a few problems, with Lea Bold (Doctor) since he did the initial examination and found (if my memory is right) no evidence of sexual activity. It is curious why Snauffer didn't tell that lie since she was telling so many others and suborning so many people. She certainly managed to suborn Dr. Lea Bold since all of a sudden we've gotten this spree of tests he "claims" was performed for gonorrhea of the mouth. That was one lie too many for Snauffer since I tested negative for gonorrhea, I couldn't have had contact with her. They'd have forged my test results too I'm sure, but (Devlin) I think really believed I had gonorrhea since I refused to take the test. She didn't see any need at the time to phony up the results. It was of course that lie that saved me instead of drowning me but it was a lie! Please check.

Well Doc that's about it for now I don't know what else I can tell you. I hope all this here seems helpful, but I've written so many letters to you and Betty about my book my head is killing me(you

see I've got arthritis you know). But let me a last quote of the bible. John 3:20 "Everyone that doeth evil hated the light either commeth to the light, lest his deeds should be reproved". So lets bring these malefactors out of the darkness and into the light. Lets expose them for the evils they've done. FIAT LUX!?!

So Gary Heidnik feels that he was framed, that he was still the victim. Heidnik explains: "I did not rape the sister of my girlfriend and didn't abduct her from Sealingsgrove I was protecting her rights".

On May 17, 1978 Alberta Davidson returned to Sealingsgrove Center with gonorrhea of the throat and vagina. Heidnik was arrested for kidnapping and rape. Upon examination, he did not have gonorrhea. To this day Heidnik maintains that he only wanted to rescue her from the institution where she was being held a prisoner. He was merely helping the sister of the women he loved.

Heidnik talked of his love for a black woman who was his common law life named Angeanette Davidson. When he speaks about Angeanette his demeanor becomes softer and he appears to be honest and believable. He did love her, I think, or did he? Heidnik called it "Love pure and simple."

It sounds wonderful but consider the following. Angeanette who's IQ was 47, became pregnant. No one saw Angeanette for months after they announced her pregnancy. Not until Betty Sizer, Angeanette's sister, paid a visit on February 22, 1978. According to Mrs. Sizer she found Angeanette eight months pregnant with sunken eyes, little or no weight gain and showing signs of physical abuse. Mrs. Sizer is an assertive women. She removed her sister and threatened Heidnik with the police.

Betty Sizer immediately took Angeanette to the hospital, Einstein Northern Division in Philadelphia. According to Mrs. Sizer, Angeanette had no prenatal care, she had gained only 5 pounds at the point when she was eight months pregnant. On the 22nd of March 1978, Angeanette delivered a 7 lb. 8 oz. baby. A large fibrous tumor prevented a normal childbirth. A Caesarean section was necessary.

Heidnik had wanted to deliver the baby at home by himself. He felt that this way was the only way he could "keep the baby". The doctors made accusations that Heidnik starved and mistreated Angeanette during her pregnancy and had denied her prenatal care. He had often given her his prescription medication.

On March 27, 1978 the Department of Public Welfare took custody of the baby. The next day Angeanette returned to live with Gary Heidnik. She received no postpartum care. Heidnik had lost his family. *It must be remembered that to Gary Heidnik family means children. Women are a means to an end a vehicle for children.*

During that year of 1978 three distinct personalities would complete their development. Heidnik when asked about the disparity of intelligence between himself and Angeanette responds that: "I didn't think it was that low." He talked about "teaching her ... about the stock market." He thought he could teach her because of the great love they had for each other, and he thought he could help her learn.

Although Heidnik had the IQ of a genius, emotionally he and Angeanette were peers. In a 1978 psychiatric exam, Donovan and Wojcietowski found that Heidnik although 34 years old, had the same dependency needs of non-demanding acceptance that most children expect from their parents.

It should be pointed out that Heidnik never received acceptance or bonding from his parents. He received discipline and abuse. The examination said "his defenses cannot tolerate

45

criticism." He was an emotional peer to the retarded women he sought out. But which Gary Heidnik was this? Gary Heidnik the bishop of his own church and a genius, or was it G.M. Kill? Who needed the closeness and acceptance?

Looking at these events of 1978 and the words of other people involved, I've discovered an answer to how Gary Heidnik, serial murderer, kept falling through the cracks of mental health institutions. In the letter reproduced at the beginning of this chapter, Heidnik explains what went on during the final days of the Alberta Davidson abduction. This letter was just one of many he had written to me explaining the events surrounding the occurrence. Trying to understand his evaluations of these events is to understand the complexities of Gary Heidnik, the "complexities" not the man.

According to Angeanette Davidson's, Gary's beloved, she like her sister Alberta had been institutionalized. She had been in a residential treatment center for the mentally retarded the Elwin Institute in Media, PA. Gary repeatedly made the point that neither her parents or any other member of their family wanted anything to do with Angeanette or Alberta while they were institutionalized.

Heidnik did not get along at all with the Davidson family. While Angeanette was living with Gary she had no apparent source of income. Gary decided to help her get social security benefits, "the biggest mistake of my life," he said later.

> Up to this time Angeanette had virtually no money and no income. There is nobody including her family especially had any interest in her. Angeanette's family did not like her and had put her into the institution at about 15 just to get rid of her. They only visited her one time in 15 years and the only reason that they visited her was to borrow money. So when Angeanette was discharged from Bellwin Institute (in Media) she had no money or

her SSI canceled because they said that she needed a guardian.

Gary Heidnik eventually helped her obtain social security benefits included with that approval was a retroactive check for more than six months payment. By the time that check for $1200 arrived Angeanette was two months pregnant. Her family did not know about the pregnancy, but they did know about the check. They offered to take her shopping and then took her to their home. It was their plan that she stay there. She telephoned Heidnik and he went over to the Davidson's home to take her back with him. They refused to allow her to go and called the police accusing Heidnik of attempting to "kidnap their retarded daughter."

The police officer asked Angeanette where she wanted to go. Angeanette replied that she wanted to go with Gary. Given the latitude of the law, she had a right to choose where she wanted to go. She went with Heidnik.

The battle between Heidnik and the Davidson's intensified. At the same time Heidnik's paranoia regarding the situation also intensified. Heidnik recalls a situation with intense detail as if it had only just happened.

> Angeanette's family being so completely venial when they heard that they lost the big check they vowed vengeance. They further learned that Angeanette was pregnant with a white man's child, it served only to add more fuel to their plans for revenge. I though I was thoroughly alerted to their nefarious intentions and behaved very circumspect. I had Angeanette in a hotel for a couple of weeks to be safe. Then when I brought her home I would not let her answer the phone when I was out and told her implicitly not to let no

one into the apartment when I was out ESPECIALLY any family members. I knew that they couldn't be trusted and that if they did snatch Angeanette again they wouldn't tell me where she was. I also knew that they wanted Angeanette very badly so if they could get their hands on her monthly SSI checks. To a large extent I over reacted, since I completely under estimated Angeanette herself she wasn't as helpless as people thought, as we were to find out.

The Davidson's feelings are perhaps understandable. They were suspicious of Heidnik and questioned his motives. Yet, they really weren't there when Angeanette needed them; Gary was. The family was angry and displeased that their daughter was pregnant. They simply didn't like it. She was retarded, she was mentally ill, so what chance would their grandchild have? The records of both 1978 and 1988 Heidnik trials indicated that he denied Angeanette prenatal care. Both the records and trial transcripts are incorrect. Not simply because of what he told me, but because of examination of documents that show she did have some prenatal care.

Since Angeanette was pregnant, I began (notice I said I began) sending her to a prenatal clinic at Pennsylvania Hospital. Occasionally I took her but I didn't have to, and Angeanette was perfectly capable of making and keeping her own appointments and often went down to 8th and Spruce on SEPTA by herself. Fortunately, there was at Pennsylvania Hospital a social worker named Patricia Lee. She was not only a so called liberated feminist, she was a local black raciest. She

> had black power pictures all over her office. When she discovered that Angeanette was living with a white man and was going to have a mixed child she was incensed. Also she further couldn't tolerate Angeanette because Angeanette was completely happy being a house wife and took very good care of her man and never gave me a difficult time. Angeanette so loved me that she would do anything I asked including having more children.

It appeared that Heidnik had finally achieved happiness and a sense of intimacy. Because he had never had it previously he needed this closeness. He could not afford to lose Angeanette. His mother had been a terrible wife to his father, she was an alcoholic, obsessive, his life as a child was tumultuous. The Heidnik family was dysfunctional with a capital D. By itself, it could provide enough material for a study in dysfunctional family groups. The pressure on Angeanette and Heidnik to abort the child was intense. Angeanette refused. There was no one in any supportive role to counsel them pervious to the pregnancy. At this point, the system began to impress its will on them. Whenever their subculture merged with society they lost. They both had been institutionalized, abandoned by family and were both paid money by society because of their deficiencies. Neither Heidnik nor Angeanette could be trusted. It was in this period that G.M. Kill was born.

As Heidnik points out the pressures on he and Angeanette intensified :

> Angeanette so loved me, she would do anything I asked, including having more children. Miss Lee couldn't tolerate such a situation and

plotted with Betty to terminate it. Miss Lee put a lot of pressure on Angeanette to leave me and to have an abortion. One time she took her out to her car told her to get in and she would find her a new home. Angeanette refused to go and informed me of what was happening.

The pressure was being put on a man with a paranoid schizophrenic diagnosis, and a mentally retarded woman. They were being told what was best for them. Back then there was no mental treatment or counseling. Let them out of the institutions, pay them, but when they breed abort them.

"All in all Angeanette did get 5 or 6 months of prenatal care before I stopped her from going."

The reason for stopping this prenatal care was clear to Heidnik. Fear of losing the baby were upper most in Heidnik's mind.

If we examine Heidnik's continuing story about Angeanette, and her family, a distinct picture of perceptual problems which relate to the Heidnik reality become obvious. There is also evidence the separation of the three Heidnik personalities.

He was first borrowing a Rolls Royce from his employer: his employer was Bishop Gary Heidnik of the United Ministers Church of Christ. Heidnik continues to talk about the story of his baby and how that eventually lead to being charged with kidnapping and rape.

As a contrast and reinforcement to what Heidnik has said in the letters reproduced in this chapter, refer to Appendix 3 which gives the cross-examination of Gary Heidnik by the prosecution in Heidnik's 1978 trial.

> We did everything and went out together everywhere. Indeed this was one of the reasons her family resented her so much, especially her sisters Betty and Bernice. They all knew they were smarter then Angeanette after all they weren't retarded right? But how come they weren't doing so well? They were all on welfare, living in the ghetto or projects and had no steady boyfriends. Betty was so desperate that she once charged her occasional friends $0.50. Talk about a cheap lay. So there they were, positively more cerebral than Angeanette but they had never been inside some of the places that Angeanette had been.

> Of course Angeanette had done something they never did ... love a white man. I not only wined and dined Angeanette but had 2 Cadillacs (a 71 Elderado and a 77 Sedan de Seville) and managed to borrow my employers Rolls Royce on several occasions. Yes her family was not only jealous but they were envious of Angeanette.

Here it can be see how Heidnik clearly delineates himself from Bishop Gary Heidnik, his employer. But Heidnik went on.

> At any rate they got hold of her again about a month before her delivery date, but Angeanette went willingly this time. I know because I found out that she was living at her sister Betty's apartment in the projects and sent in the police. The police came out and asked if she wanted to stay. Angeanette said yes and so I backed off. Surprisingly Angeanette managed to contact me

one time by a trick even I never thought of. She called me collect. I never even considered calling anyone collect unless it was long distance so I learned something from her. She said she was at the hospital at the University of Pennsylvania with Betty so I went right over. Angeanette still refused to come home with me but we had a nice talk...

Heidnik never responded as to why Angeanette went away so willingly. Perhaps all was not so wonderful as it appeared to him. Here again we see Heidnik slipping through the cracks in the system. If he was abusive and gave Ms. Davidson prescription drugs why was that never an issue for the courts?

The physicians at the hospital of the University of Pennsylvania are among the best in the country. They certainly would have filed abuse petitions for the welfare of Angeanette and the baby. I have never uncovered those petitions.

At this time the full personalities of Gary Heidnik were not developed. The incidents were significant in making Heidnik more cunning. The expert of manipulation does not seem present in March of 1978. But perhaps the question of how Heidnik and others like him become experts of manipulation is. Is it what they have to do to survive in normal society? Or is it because they see the rules and authority figures of the normal world as being there only to punish? These questions, of course, cannot really be answered. But the events do show problems with our social welfare system. It also partly explains the birth of the third Heidnik personality, G. M. Kill.

CHAPTER 5

THE FANTASY IS THE MOTIVE

In Heidnik's fantasy, in his dreams and delusions, were the motives for his sex slaves, the tortures and the murders. His fantasy began to take control in 1978 when two major events changed his life forever. Both of these events were explained in the previous chapters. The first was when his common law wife Angeanette Davidson gave birth to Ann Davidson. The daughter who was promptly taken away from them by the Department of Public Welfare. The second was when Angeanette visited her institutionalized, retarded sister Alberta and signed her out on a four hour pass and then never returned her. Alberta, as we said, was subsequently found in a coal bin in the basement of Heidnik's apartment.

Heidnik spent 5 years in the prison system. He also spent additional time in mental health facilities for the criminally insane. During the time that he was in psychiatric wards, he was away from women and sex. He had only his financial pages, and his hyper-sex drive to consume him. Masturbating behaviors increased and he needed dominance fantasies to fuel his sex drive. He had made a mistake with Alberta. She was subservient, retarded like a three year old, but she had been missed by the institution. Heidnik needed to be physically

dominant over the women.

Upon release from prison in 1983 Heidnik moved himself and his fantasies to West Philadelphia. Some of his belongings would later be described as "cases of various pornography." Gary fueled his fantasy with objects, magazines and movies. To a normal person, pornography may serve only for sexual arousal. But for Heidnik it was more, it was fuel, but it was not enough.

His internal world needed control over more than just magazines and movies. He suppressed this as much as he could with his church and his good deeds. Heidnik was however, slowly losing the war for his soul. The fantasy, the need for control and for acceptance could not be suppressed forever.

In Heidnik's mind, it was a war between God and Satan for the possession of his soul. Part of him felt guilty and ashamed of his fantasy and then he would try to do more for the church, for the retarded, and for the handicapped. He took boarders into his house. He traded his house and financial well being for their companionship and friendship. One of the boarders Sandra Lindsay. She would die in his basement 4 years later. They were friends.

Sandra Lindsay visited Heidnik when he was in the hospital after his February 1986 suicide attempt. She liked and trusted him. Yet in November 1987, Sandra Lindsay became his second prisoner and his first victim.

According to Gary it was not his fault, and he can't imagine how she died. "Also she wasn't standing all that long, that particular time. A hour and a half to be exact. She spent the previous night standing about 12 hours without ill effect," he said.

When speaking of Sandra Lindsay's ordeal in the basement, Heidnik neglects to mention that she was on a diet of

bread and water, had a chest cold, and was clothed only in a shirt. His perception of why someone on a cold February day, in a damp earth basement, and without sleep for at least one evening, might choke to death after being forcibly fed bread and water, is clearly impaired.

In Heidnik's world he was in control, all the women, including Sandra Lindsay, were under his care. So her dying was only an inconvenient mystery to him.

He was casually watching T.V. upstairs in the Church of the United Ministers of God, while six naked women were chained in the basement. Listen to Heidnik's words:

> I don't know exactly what day it was but it was in February. A movie with Linda Lavin in Australia started about 8 or 9 o'clock and that was when I stood her up. After a hour and a half the movie wasn't over yet, they broke for a commercial, I went downstairs and Sandy was hanging by her arm, her legs bent and her head rolled to one side.

> There was no willful intent or premeditation on my part to kill anyone. As a matter of fact, the actual causes of there deaths was ambiguous, regardless of what the corner [sic] said. He claimed it was murder since the body was mutilated.

> Bull s _ _ _!! Nobody knows how she died. She may have strangled on a piece of food or had a heart attack or maybe a stroke. Nobody knows,

but it WAS NOT MURDER!! The witnesses even testified I wasn't in the same room even at the actual time of death. They also testified that I didn't strangle, stab, shoot or anything else. Declaring a pair of handcuffs as the murder weapon is preposterous. Nobody <u>deliberately</u> kills someone with a pair of handcuffs. If you want to DELIBERATELY kill someone you use a gun or a knife or something. And my purposes were to create life with lots of babies; not to take lives.

This was the death that still puzzles him to this day. In fact, the exact cause of Sandra Lindsay *is* a mystery. Her body was dismembered.

As Heidnik puts it, there were actually "3 deaths at 3520 North Marshall not 2. When Sandy died she was about 2 months pregnant, so two people died that day."

He dismembered the body for a reason. He told two defense psychiatrists that he stored the arms and legs in the freezer/refrigerator "to feed to the babies when they were born." His sexual delusions were over-powering. If what Heidnik told these psychiatrists is accurate, it is obvious that when he discovered that Sandra was pregnant during the dismemberment, he did not simply throw the fetus away. Upon cutting her stomach from the top of the rib cage to pass the navel, he removed the fetus, his child. The child was dead but no one would take it from him this time. He laid the child down on the table and watched it while he continued his laborious task of hacking Sandra Lindsay, the mother, apart. He cooked the fetus and fed it with rice to the hostages. No one took his baby away this time. As he cooked the torso, head and body of Sandra Lindsay, he kept what was his to do with as he deemed fit. In his internal world he was the deity.

Investigators found no blood at the crime scene after an exhaustive search. There was no blood was found in any room. The investigators disassembled the traps and sewer pipes from the house all the way to the external sewer line. Samples were taken from the entire assembly, however they found no blood.

The answer to what happened to the blood comes from an analysis of interviews with Gary Heidnik. It is important to analyze Heidnik's thought process. Heidnik is logical, methodical and very patient. As we have see from his own words, he thinks through every move he makes. Since his actual life has been an internal life, he is at his best when he is in his own internal world. Therefore, it is likely that he rehearsed the disposal of the body frequently *prior* to the actual attempt of the dismemberment of Sandra Lindsay.

Immediately after Sandra Lindsay's death, Heidnik put her body into the freezer and turned on every cold water spigot in the house. He had, in his garage, a small engine hoist he had used for automobile repairs. He disassembled the engine hoist and moved it into the bathroom. He reassembled it as a "body hoist" and mounted it over the bath tub.

After allowing the body to freeze much like in a mortuary, Heidnik brought the body upstairs. He drained the body of its blood and fluids over the bath tub. Blood does not coagulate in cold water, as Heidnik the licensed practical nurse and avid reader with a superior intellect would have known. Blood would also leave no trace in the traps or pipes because the pipes were chilled. It would move through them all into the sewer line. No blood traces could be found in the cold pipes or the bath tub. The body was hoisted to allow a downward drain of the blood from the specific areas where it collects on a dead body dependent upon the position of the body in death. These simple logical steps provide an explanation as to why no blood was found. Perhaps more importantly, they show that the scene had been rehearsed over and over in Heidnik's

fantasy until the details were perfected.

Heidnik could no longer distinguish his fantasy world from reality. His internal world had *become* the external world. He was in control. Beginning in 1978, Heidnik began to move his internal fantasy into the external world. The fantasy began to be more than an internal masturbating fantasy fueled by dreams and a large supply of vengeance. Vengeance against the system, against the external world, against society and against those who were in control. In his perception those in authority, took his wife, his child, and his happiness. People in control were always taking things. His mother and father took his innocence, and his childhood. Closeness, bonding, and intimacy were replaced by anger, aggression and control.

FANTASY - DELUSION, HALLUCINATION?

In 1983 as Heidnik's need for intimacy was not met by his wife Betty. His sexual needs grew. To be precise, in Heidnik's case, it is important to realize that this need is actually more of a drive. A drive is almost primitive or instinctual. It is more then just a need. It is an overwhelming thrust born of repetitive fantasy.

Each individual fantasy is eventually worn out in masturbating behavior, but gives further fuel to the internal life and therefore even more is needed to achieve orgasm. As it achieves orgasm each new and individual fantasy must out due the previous one until a fantasy is reached that involves total control. Once this is achieved, the fantasy must then be active during masturbation or sexual intercourse in order to achieve orgasm. This is a repetitive, consistent drive.

The Heidnik fantasy became reality with a partner, Josephina Rivera. It seems likely that Rivera would do anything that Heidnik wanted in order to avoid punishment. It was she who suggested sex slaves. This would coincide perfectly with

Heidnik's internal world, where pregnancy would be the ultimate control. It would give him control or lordship over his victims. The fantasy could then become almost primitively ritualistic by nature. Heidnik became the item of worship or a god in his internal world.

A god has control. Heidnik, like other serial murders, have control and become gods with unlimited power. In this experience then, anything they do is okay, so long as it is part of the ritual of worship. This includes death, torture, necrophilia, etc.

Perhaps early in life, things other than regular sexual intercourse crept into his sexual fantasies and aroused him. Possibly he masturbated to the fantasy of women in chains or other similar slave fantasies. It is impossible to know.

Whatever the fantasies, they escalated into a instinctual drives that had to be fulfilled. Thirst with drink, hunger with food, sex with intercourse and control with slaves.

Heidnik talked as if God wanted him to have children and babies. The voice in his head was not God. The voice was his subconscious, and it had given him directions. The subconscious that had been fed control as a substitute for intimacy. Eventually, his subconscious confused his fantasies and his own inner voice with that of a deity. His fantasies eventually gained control of his entire being. The potential part of this fantasy, the one that would fuel the continuing internal experience, was that he was making life better for his victims. If he made things better for them, they owed him. If they owed them, eventually he would own them. They became his possessions. Possessions to be used as he pleased, and in Heidnik's world if they owed him they were merely objects to be used to intensify any of his desires which might relate to any of his fantasies.

Heidnik viewed this much in the same way as purchasing a "blow-up doll" in a sex shop. Heidnik's dream was one of con-

trol, dominance and lordship. It was one of a god. *The motive for his actions in the basement of his Marshall Street apartment was his dream.* Keeping the women pregnant was a form of control. There was no choice for the women, none. The likelihood of any of the women lasting the full term of pregnancy was almost nil.

When Sandra Lindsay choked to death Heidnik tasted blood for the first time. It escalated his fantasy. It began a new SRS cycle. He had achieved the ultimate form of control ... death. But death is only a form of control for a human being. A god can control an individual even after death.

The point reached in the basement of that apartment in Philadelphia, as we have been pointing out, was not something that happened over night. Gary's internal life began at an early age. He was not socially accepted by children in the neighborhood. He spent a lot of time alone, according to his brother Terry: "Other kids made fun of him and called him football head."

It was in fantasies that Gary Heidnik learned that he could be in control. In the external world he was at the mercy of others. He was intelligent, but perceived as an odd ball. His father neglected him, and was simultaneously a stern disciplinarian. His father was a simple person, and Gary's eccentricities and intelligence may have threatened him. He therefore became overly critical and physically abusive, perhaps to demonstrate his authority and control. As with all human beings, Gary Heidnik needed acceptance and understanding. The only place he was sure to receive these, was in his own internal world.

As he reached puberty, his sexual drives began to awaken and the fantasy life took on new aspects. In the external world, he remained the introvert who had almost no contact with the opposite sex. His desire for acceptance and a place in the external world took him on an odyssey to Staughten Military Academy. Eventually, this same need supplied the courage he

needed to enlist in the army. Heidnik chose the military police. The selection was made to place him above those who had enlisted with him. It was a certain path to acceptance, and an accelerated path to control. MP's carry a great deal of power and control over other soldiers. But Gary never became an MP. Authority decided for him. The Army made him a medic.

A secondary motivation for his enlistment was an attempt to gain control of himself through discipline that the military service can offer. The regiment of training allowed him to gain control of the fantasy, or the world within his head.

Still, his mind would race on. He would spend hours deliberating about the fantasies of his internal life. When at times, he could not tell the internal fantasies from the external world, psychologists would call them hallucinations and grandiose delusions. At times Gary Heidnik was aware, and did know that his fantasies were gaining control over him. During one of these times, he chose enlistment.

In the army, after training ends, a soldier is given a job. This job is often commonplace and of the 9 to 5 variety, when not at war or the soldier does not have a critical position. The job is often that of nothing more than an orderly, regardless of what it is called, or as Heidnik called it "a glorified gopher." At this point Gary's external structure was moved to Landsthul, Germany. He was having difficulty coping with his internal world which was interfering with his functioning in the external world. In three months he was again losing control and had to be hospitalized. He wet the bed, was nauseous, dizzy and developed ticks. He also flirted with the idea of suicide. He discovered that suicide was a way to stop his mind from racing.

It was the beginning of a pattern. When he could not differentiate his internal and external world he would be hospitalized in psychiatric institutions. This happened 22 more times. As time went on, Heidnik could not find a way to gain

closeness, acceptance or control. He could not control himself or anyone else for that matter. His difficulty was due in part to his hyper-sexual drive. It eventually ended up as the horrific crime on Marshall Street in Philadelphia. He committed those acts without a guilty conscience, or with any remorse. From his description of the deaths, it is obvious that the women involved were mere objects. Objects to be manipulated and changed to fit his delusional needs. In fact, he wasn't interested in babies or children either. That was an manipulation. He was only interested in having women that fit his needs. They were objects to be manipulated to fulfill his intimacy/control needs.

CHAPTER 6

VICTIM SELECTION

The selection of victims by the serial murderer is difficult to discern, in that it is based *entirely* on internal delusional fantasies. The selection of victims by Gary Heidnik is a case in point. To add to the confusion, there may be certain characteristics that the victims have in common, that *appear* to suggest a traditional motive. Using these common characteristics, law enforcement officials begin to hunt for the killer. Although the common characteristics seem to describe a motive and aid in the search, the actual fact is that apprehension of a serial killer may take longer. *The motive generally apparent to law enforcement officials may not be the motive at all.*

Ressler, Burgess and Douglas (1988) delineate two types of murderers, each of which selected different victims. They detail murders with a plan, and those without a plan. For the murderer with a conscious plan or fantasy, selecting the victim begins the acting-out level of behavior. The plan or fantasy, constructed earlier, may call for a victim who meets certain criteria, and many murderers have been known to seek out a victim who is exactly right for their fantasy.

Gary Heidnik was one who had a conscious plan. He sought mostly black women with a borderline IQ. His plan was to find women who would be submissive, who would bear him children. He searched for women that he could control.

When investigating potential serial killers, law enforcement officials should compare the characteristics of the missing people, within the area. The histories of the known victims, when correlated, *may* provide a profile for potential victims. To correlate such information, start with a basic description and the physical characteristics of know victims. These characteristics should include race, sex, hair and eye color. Other obvious traits and characteristics should also be noted. What also must not be overlooked or minimized are areas the victims frequented, activities, and hobbies. *In other words, the victims should be profiled as carefully as the FBI National Center for Analysis of Violent Crime - Violent Criminal Apprehension Program [VICAP], profiles the serial killer.*

The work begun by Robert Ressler to profile the killers must and will always remain. But a similar thoroughness needs to be implemented in the characterization of known victims. It can help identify and protect potential victims, as well as lead to the apprehension of the killer.

It is possible, that if we profile victims with the detail of VICAP methodology, part of the motive, which is the fantasy of the serial killer may become apparent. This information, combined with the FBI profile of the killer, could provide law enforcement personnel with a tool to apprehend the murderer while he is still in "full bloom."

In the case of Gary Heidnik, the victims were all caught by Heidnik using similar means. The parents of Sandra Lindsay reported her missing. There were other reports of missing persons who turned out to be Heidnik victims. Although all police departments are inundated with such reports, a victim profile, coupled with a correlation of missing persons in the area, may have been able to find Heidnik in mid-fantasy.

Ressler, Burgess and Douglas also identify another type of killer, one without a plan or conscious fantasy. This type of serial killer may select victims based on the kind of response they elicit in certain circumstances.

For example, someone may remind him of his belief in an unjust world. He may feel unfairly treated, and this sets into motive for his justification to kill. One killer felt that his continued rejection by women was an injustice. In response to his frustrations over this feeling, he shot and killed women who were either accompanied by men, or were attractive enough to be sought by men. Other murderers respond to victims with rage and anger.

Harrison Marty Graham met both criteria. He had a fantasy of himself as a demonic predator, as demonstrated by some of his sketches, reproduced below from photocopies of the originals.

It is possible that he saw the demon within himself, and he first murdered after being rejected by Robin DeShadis. She had let him know that she no longer wanted to be with him. Graham convinced her to stay through R's & T's, Ritilin and Taulin, and had sex with her one final time. Upon climax, he choked her. She never left him. Later, he continued to have intercourse with her body. She was found mummified in his closet wrapped in a green garbage bag. She never left him until all his horrors were eventually discovered in North Philadelphia.

Ressler and Shactman in their book *Whoever Fights Monsters*, talk about organized and disorganized crimes. In the book,

Ressler's work with the FBI Behavioral Sciences Unit is expanded with regard to the effort to characterize serial killers. Ressler defines, and I agree, organized crimes as premeditated, not crimes that are spur of the moment. The planning and the crimes are acted out behaviors drawn from fantasies that may be developed over years.

Gary Heidnik was an organized offender. As is seen from the words of Gary Heidnik, reported throughout this book, he was a clear documented organized offender. The fantasy was nurtured, reinforced and finally acted out. The organized offender, such as Heidnik, personalizes the victims he eventually interacted with and recognized them as individuals prior to capturing them.

Ressler further defines the disorganized killers as those who do not choose their victims logically. They have no interest in the personality of their victims. This kind of a killer wants nothing at all to do with the personality of the victim. The disorganized killer is one who is usually alone and has totally and actively rejected society.

The organized offender, such as Gary Heidnik, tend to keep trophies of their victims to reinforce and fuel their ritualistic fantasies. Thus when examining a crime scene, it is imperative that any missing body parts, clothes, rings, wallets, ID's, jewelry, photographs or any missing object, particularly things that seem out of the ordinary be identified. They are important. These missing items, may be the *trophies* of the serial killer, but they are also invaluable clues to law enforcement officials in the identification of the serial killer's motive. *They are a real world insight into the fantasy.* Similar missing items in what may seem to be unrelated cases, particularly in the same geographic area, may be the only signal that there is a serial killer operating.

It should be noted that the missing items may not necessarily be expensive. They will be items that are necessary to the killer to keep the excitement of the event alive to the killer. In

behavioral terminology, they are "cues" that have reinforcing qualities. They allow successful re-enactment for the killer and provide fantasy driven reinforcement of the crime on an ongoing basis.

The basis for keeping these articles is not robbery, that is not the motive. They are not normal clues. The missing item(s) can provide law enforcement with a first probe into the mind of the serial killer.

This can also be seen quite clearly by Wesley Dodd's answer to Alan Austin's on PBS' *Frontline* [11/10/92] question of why Dodd kept a photo album.

> Two reasons, really. One was to help me remember what I had done, exactly what happened, what he looked like, for my own, you know, pleasure, and to look at the photos later on. And another one was so the next time I got a boy home, I could show him pictures of Lee hanging in the closet and then I'd kill that boy.

This lack of a typical motive, based on apparent common traits among victims, is often baffling to many law enforcement officers. Often it appears as if victim selection was random; sometimes with only loose connections among the victims. For example, all of the victims maybe women who are white with brown hair, or they maybe all black, or all males of a certain age, etc. But to the serial killer each victim meets exact and rigid specifications.

Each selection is made in order to further fuel the internal fantasy. Certainly there are at times careless selections or mistakes, changes to the apparent pattern yet on the whole the selection is specific. There may be a deviation from their pattern may cause a chain of errors that eventually lead to their capture. Josephine Rivera was often used by Gary Heidnik to help him identify and select victims. Heidnik would promise Rivera

extra food, or bring her upstairs and let her watch a movie, if she agreed to help him. At times, she even talked to the victims prior to Heidnik actually picking them up she let them know that Gary was okay.

Gary Heidnik's selection was not random. He'd carefully approach, talk to, have intercourse with, and then choke his victims. He looked for certain subservient qualities in the women he chose. He selected women, who in his fantasies, he could rationalize to himself would be better off with him in his basement than with their own families. They were usually women who accepted gifts without question, and who were generally of low intelligence. These women had little positive family support. It should be noted that Heidnik took several women back to his house for sex, *and did not attempt to capture them.* That was the detailed selection process at work.

In addition, there was an absolute *ritual* to the experience. Heidnik would begin by taking them to dinner, then back to his house for a movie. Then, after conversation, maybe a drink and he would put on a porn movie. After this, he would take them into a back room for sex. It was only at this point that Heidnik would make his final decision as to whether the woman would become one of his victims. If they were chosen, he would choke them into unconsciousness, and take them into the basement and chain and handcuff them.

On December 22, 1987, Lisa Thomas was walking to her friend's house on Lehigh Avenue, near 8th and Cambria in Philadelphia. She noticed a brand new black and gray Cadillac as it drove by.

By the second time this car had circled the block, she had already decided to wave at the driver. She gave her reason for this action, she said; "I liked the car." Lisa didn't realize that her decision to be friendly would change her life forever. The driver of that brand new car was Gary Heidnik. Heidnik was in the process of looking for his third sex slave.

"When he stopped and rolled down the window, I walked over to the car. He said: 'Do you want to see my prick?' And he exposed himself. I told him I was not a prostitute."

These are Lisa Thomas' words about her first encounter with Gary Heidnik. Yet the actions did not deter Lisa. Heidnik asked where she was going, and she told him to a friend's house. When he asked if he could drive her, she agreed. He took her to her friends where Lisa got to show-off in the new car.

"Then he took me to TGIF's out on City Line. He bought me my first martini." Lisa went on to relate how Heidnik then took her to Sears and spent $50 on new clothes for her. Heidnik then went on to the next step in the ritual.

"After that, he took me home and we watched a movie, *Splash*, then we went upstairs and had sex. We were laying there naked and he stood up, went behind me, and started choking me. He had cuffed my arms behind my back and then took me downstairs." Victim three had been found.

She remembered being too terrified to resist. She was naked, handcuffed and he threatened to beat her if she put up any resistance.

"On the way downstairs, I saw some white bags, and I thought: 'I bet there are body parts in those bags,' " she said.

"He took me into the basement, and told me he wanted me to meet his friends. He went over to this plywood board with sandbags on it, and removed the sand bags. Two girls came up with only shirts on...with no bottoms." Lisa Thomas, now thoroughly terrified, did notice that the women were chained to a pipe in the ceiling. She also noticed a portable toilet and a dirty mattress. He told the women to help chain Lisa to the ceiling. Lisa said that Heidnik used a muffler clamp attached to her wrist, and that she had enough chain to move, but only slightly.

The fantasy was now in full control. Heidnik told her, "I want you to kiss my ass." She said she bent over and kissed his "butt." She also had to tell him that he was the "boss." She was told that he would feed her only bread and water for a few days, until she learned to do what he wanted.

As with Lisa Thomas, Heidnik always tried to judge his victims carefully. He was interested in women that he thought he could control, and that could bear children. He told Lisa that he wanted: "... ten children...and you will deliver Indian style...if you bleed, I can't help you, I'm not a doctor."

The common factors in all the victims was the control and child bearing. Other similarities in the victims were in a sense accidental. He had sex with several other women, while the victims were chained in the basement. These women were not chosen as victims. *Heidnik looked for women that he perceived needed him.* These women had very little in the way of possessions and he thought he could control them in this way. He rationalized that he was giving them a better life. The fantasy was about *control*, but to Heidnik, it was *intimacy*.

During intercourse with these women, he would have the ones that were selected to be his victims assume the top position while with those he did not select he would usually end up in the bottom position. In a normal mind, the top or bottom position during intercourse need not symbolize any control, but in Heidnik's mind it did. It was the last bit of freedom he would let these women express.

When chained in the basement, the women would be beaten until they told him "you're the boss Gary", and would have to, as Lisa Thomas describes "kiss his ass, literally" and at the same time they would have to tell him he was in charge. Then he forced them to engage in oral sex with him.. always culminating in vaginal sex. This pattern was repeated every day on a cot in front of the other hostages. These sexual encounters all began with the *control ritual.*

This ritual would always include initial oral sex then vaginal intercourse. Heidnik enjoyed participating in group sex as well. He would often ejaculate while having oral sex, when that happened, he would instruct one of the women to "get his juice." He was always in control and dominant.

The fact that he was often involved in group sex, and often would ejaculate during any sex, helps demonstrate that his concern was not simply procreating as "god told him." He needed control, dominance and leadership. He became the god of his own fantasy.

The only deviation in his selection process was Josephine Rivera. She helped fuel his fantasy. She was attractive, and was eventually put in charge of the other women. Heidnik gave her the most privileges.

She was in fact "mistress of the dungeon." She appeared to accept him, and enjoyed the sexual experience most. Rivera was fuel for the fantasy. According to Lisa Thomas, she was always given special treatment.

Also, according to Thomas, Rivera was a "rat" who would always tell Heidnik anything the prisoners might be thinking of trying. The result would be privileges for Rivera and torture for one of the others. Rivera was accepted by Heidnik and allowed to go out to dinner with Gary and generally had the run of the place. She would also, with Heidnik, initiate some of the torture inflicted on the other women.

Lisa Thomas has said that it was Rivera who had applied the electric shock to Debra Dudley on the day she died. But, it was this deviation from this selection process that lead to his capture. Rivera outsmarted Heidnik by giving the appearance and pleading to Heidnik's sexual vanities.

Heidnik's perception of women is clarified when we look at the thoughts he expressed in a letter to his wife, Betty Ditso. [Note, the punctuation, spelling and syntax, as in all the let-

ters, are Heidnik's}

Although some of the original letter has been lost, what was left is still revealing. It reads:

(This is to be the final chapter honey)

Betty

If someone were ever to analyze me; you know, disect me, take me apart and examine me under a microscope, and then put me back together, and then when he made his report, he tried to condense it in as few words as possible it would probably read something like this; "He used non-traditional means to solve his problems." As a matter of fact when I die, they'll probably write on my tombstone something like this:

HERE LIES
GARY M. HEIDNIK
"A NON-TRADITIONAL
SORT OF GUY'
1943-19...

So in true personal style, when it comes to finding a life mate (wife) I approached the situation in unorthodox fashion. It all started with a newspaper column. The writer told about this individual who started a pen pal club, so American men could meet, and perhaps marry Oriental women. In this way he'd be responsible for several hundred marriages.
They also listed the address of this penpals club. I had seen the movie, "The World of Suzy Wong" about five times and seen all those pictures of the

dutiful Japanese wives licking off their husbands shoes and never giving any back talk. Always answering with a "Yes dear, No dear, Anything you say dear."...

CHAPTER 7

THE MANIPULATOR

Heidnik learned in about 1978, that he had a great capacity for the art of manipulation. As long as his internal world remained internal and did not encroach on his conscious world, he could certainly manipulate. Heidnik had to learn to control his external world to fit his overpowering internal world. Manipulation became his alley. As he said himself, "I'm crazy not stupid."

Heidnik used his intelligence to outsmart those around him. Heidnik attempted to be one step ahead of everyone. He learned to manipulate to survive. He learned to manipulate people in his external world, so as they would not interfere with his fantasies. Important things were arranged out of convenience, appearance or the mask of sanity. But they were arranged by Heidnik to avoid discovery, capture or interference. The internal fantasy was in control.

Heidnik, like all other serial killers, arranged the external world to keep the fantasy alive. He would hold church services for his handicapped parishioners while he kept women chained in his basement. He was in control, as a bishop in control of his handicapped and dependent flock, and as the ritualistic killer in control of his slaves. Listen to the words Gary Heidnik used to describe some of his church members:

> As you may know, my church was almost exclusively comprised of the handicapped. It was never intended to be a church for the handicapped. It just happened that way. The handicapped are more comfortable socially with other handicapped and picked a church they could attend without fear of ridicule. This is a vacuum in your mainline churches, and I inadvertently filled it. I did little actual preaching at the church, I let others do the ministering. I simply acted like a guide and tried to gently keep things on track.

Heidnik knew that if he didn't continue to manipulate and control, the fantasy would end. He thought that the greater amount of control he could render, the greater the chance would be that he could fulfill his goal. The goal of his own family and a Heidnik dominated society.

In fact, when he lost control of Rivera, it did actually all end. The choice of Rivera was, as mentioned, a miscalculation. *Often, when lost in the fantasy, the serial killer makes a mistake in the world of reality.* The delusional based thinking is often muddled, on the level of the real world because the fantasy is all-consuming. When the desire becomes so overpowering that the killer needs to reinforce the fantasy by acting out through manipulation, the killer can miscalculate. *In effect, the killer manipulates himself into believing that he can outsmart everyone in the external world.* It is this self-manipulation, this thinking, this response pattern that often leads to the apprehension of the serial killer.

Once their fantasy is realized, and they need to continue, they become smug, superior, and convince themselves that they are invincible. Bishop Gary of the United Ministers of

Christ, thought he was a deity, above all others, able to manipulate us mortal's to fulfill his inner needs. He was successful in fulfilling this part of his fantasy. But as Gacy, Graham and others, he crashed headlong into the real world, landing on Death Row.

We know that a serial killer must control events. In order to exercise this control, to actually be in control, the killer must manipulate. The killer will manipulate people, places, and events to fit his fantasy. The killer usually knows what he is doing, even makes some apparently rational decisions, but, he is driven by the need to engage in the fantasy behavior. Therefore the serial killer can make and keep doctor's appointments and even be examined by psychiatrists and psychologists. Heidnik and others, have often appeared "normal" in these self-report evaluations.

The serial killers are often able to out-manipulate and out-think even the best trained mental health professionals. The serial killer will do whatever is necessary to keep the fantasy alive. They know that failure to respond will lead to mistakes, and that these mistakes will lead to capture. To be in control is to be powerful, and the power over life and death is the ultimate manipulation. This manipulation is what the serial killer seeks.

Ressler, et. al. (pg. 217) reproduce a letter from John Gacy to a female friend that was originally published by the *Chicago Sun Times*. Part of the letter states:

> The state said that I was manipulative or a manipulator. Hell yes. But had I not been, I would not have been successful. You wouldn't be successful undercover if you didn't manipulate at times.

It is any wonder why Ressler refers to organized murderers as "manipulative geniuses," that can fool psychiatrists or other mental health professionals?

Gary Heidnik manipulated to bring his internal fantasy world into the external Heidnik reality. Some of his more clear manipulations were:

- Forced Sandra Lindsay to write a letter to her parents telling them that she was okay, and would be away for a while. He then drove to New York to mail the letter.

- Dumped Debra Dudley's body in a park in New Jersey. He forced Josephine Rivera to accompany him, and assist in the body dispersal.

- Chopped Sandra Lindsay's body and disposed of the blood and body parts by dismembering them and cooking and feeding the parts to his other "sex slaves."

- When police came to his house to check out a reported odor, Heidnik convinced them that he had burned a roast. The odor had been reported as being detectable for two days, it took a great deal of manipulation to convince the officers that he had been cooking a roast for 48 hours.

- Heidnik let his other victims know that they had eaten Sandra Lindsay's body to assure control over them. He openly tortured them, and had them beat each other to avoid punishment.

- He faked leaving the house, and if the women in the basement made noise, or attempted to escape they would be punished. One such punishment was to puncture their eardrums with a screw drivert without the ability to hear, that way, the victims would never

know whether he was home or not.

- He fooled 150 to 200 psychiatrists, psychologists and other mental health professionals.

- He made Josephine Rivera assist in victim selection and capture.

- The church and those he had as his parishioners and "board of directors" were controlled by Bishop Gary.

Gary Heidnik was often accused of being a malingerer. He was not. *He is a manipulator.* He manipulated everyone and everything around him to maintain his fantasy. Even after his capture, I, at times, fell victim to his manipulation. I often needed to step back and objectively review the words and the data.

It is important that no mental health professional rely on self-report in these cases. Instead we must rely on records, legal information, and any hard data that may be available, without which we can become as vulnerable (maybe more so) to manipulation as anyone.

Delusional drive is over powering, instinctual, and in control. The internal world arranges things in the external world for its survival. This is the same instinctual survival drive that all animals possess. Any authority or dominant figure that could interrupt Heidnik's internal world was manipulated. Heidnik attempted this crazy act on the arresting officers who interrogated him.

In that interview, he gave what was an average performance jumping from one item to another, never acknowledging what was in his basement or in his freezer. The actual words from transcript of the arrest is shown in the box on the next eight pages.

**Statement taken from Gary M Heidnik
assigned by Cpl. Withers 5:30AM 03-25-87**

Signed

P/O R.A. Young #5735

1. Q. Do you understand that you have a right to keep quiet, and do not have to say anything at all?

A. Yes.

2. Q. Do you understand that anything you say can and will be used against you?

A. Yes.

3. Q. Do you want to remain silent?

A. No.

4. Q. Do you understand that you have a right to talk with a lawyer before we ask you any questions?

A. Yes.

5. Q. Do you understand that if you cannot afford to hire a lawyer, and you want one, we will not ask you any questions until a lawyer is appointed for you free of charge.

A. Yes.

6. Q. Do you want to talk with a lawyer at this time, or to have a lawyer with you while we ask you questions?

A. No, I'll talk to you.

7. Q. Are you willing to answer questions of your own free will, without force or fear, and without any threats or promises having been made to you?

A. Yes.

Statement of Gary M. Heidnik Date: 03-25-87 /5:30AM
(Refused to Sign) P/O R.A. Young #5735 (signed)

Cpl. G. Withers #8204 SCU-1   SCU-1-D

Case No 1148

Interviewer: P/O R.A. Young #5735

Name: Gary Michael Heidnik

Age: 43 Race: W/M DOB: 11/22/43

Address 3324 "A" St./3520 N. Marshall St.

Phone No. 228-3266

Name of Employment/School: Unemployed

Soc. Sec. No. 220-66-986

Address of Employment/School: none

Dates of planned vacations: None

Dates of planned business trips: none

Place of interview SCU Date 03—25—87

Time 5:30 AM

Brought in by Police Date 03—25—87

Time 1:00 AM

We are questioning you concerning Incidents at 3520 N. Marshall St.

Warnings given by P/O R.A.Young #5735 SCU-1-D

Date 03—2587 Time 5:30AM

Answers :

(1)Yes (2) Yes (3) No (4) Yes (5) Yes (6) No (7) Yes

Gary I'M P/O Young #5735 I'm gonna question you on matters reported to the Phila. Police Sex Crimes Unit and I'm going to type in your responses to my questioning herein.

Q/1: Do you know why you are here in the Sex Crimes Unit?

A.1: Non-Support. Yeah, that's why I'm here.

Q/2: What about the girls Gary?

A.2: I don't know what you're talking about.

Q/3: Do you want to tell me what happened at your house with these girls?

A.3: I ain't gonna pat that bitch is not going to get a dime out of me. That bitch is laying other guys and I'm supposed to support her.

Q.4: What girl? Whats her name?

A.4: What's her name, that things in court i don't want to get involved by that that's in court.

Q.5: Is she white or black?

A.5: You ain't gonna trick me.

Q.6: I'm not trying to trick you Gary.

A.6: Can I have some coffee?

Q.7: Yes, here it is Gary.

A.7: She named her kid after her boyfriend. Ands I'm supposed to pay her support.

Q.8: Gary I really don't know her name, who are you talking about?

A.8: Look your going to find I'm a tough nut to crack, I'm not going to pay.

Q.9: What about your house Gary, what happened there?

A.9: I put up some new cabinets, in the kitchen.

Q.10: What about the basement?

A:10: What about the basement I put the cabinets in the kitchen.

Q.11: They found body parts in the refrig. do you know that?

A:11: I'm supposed to pay her $135.00 per week to her and I am not paying shit. She's laying with a guy named John, You see these pictures, the pictures are over by my wallet, the kid is mine, I'm not sure. I;'m getting a blood test, And I'm supposed to support a person like that..Here let me show you the pictures this kid is cute but I'm not sure he's mine. This is a boy Jesse John Heidnik The same last name as mine.

Q.12: Is he white or black?

A.12: Let's just say he's not white.

Q.13: Is his mom white?

A.13: I'm not even white. I'm mixed you know what a Creole is I'm from Miss. I got a little black and indian in me.

Q.14: Is your wife up here?

A.14: She had to file a file a petition to for me to be here.

Q.15: What about the women chained up in your house?

A.15: Your like a broken record, I don't blame you for laughing, now your smiling. This is your story you tell me, you'll make this up you guys will do anything to get a guy today.

Q.16: Is your wife in N.J.?

A.16: You got to understand me I'm not going to pay you can lock me up and throw away the key I'm not paying.

Q.17: Your mad at your wife, huh?

A.17: You got that right.

Q.18: Your child is 1/2 white and Black.

A.18: I guess, I don't even know the percentage I have in me.

Q.19: Are you mad at the girls who are at the house?

A.19: You know that story again, It's your story.

Q.20: What do you have in the refrigerator?

A.20: Bread Soda, Ice Cubes, Pickles Olives. Hamburgers, Hot Dogs, its a frigedare there really good. Whirlpool sucks, I almost bought one.

Q.21: What about body parts?

A.22: That's supposed to make me pay you telling stories like that.

Q.23: Did you cut up anybody?

A.23: No your unbelievable, I'm ridiculous. I like that. I see how you do that.

Q.24: A girl named Rivera came in here and said you kept you there at your house? Nice looking girl right?

A.24: Its gotta be better than my wife. Huh, huh you guys already know. I caught you in that one.

Q.25: Did you just buy a car?

A.25: Oh know you don't you ain't takin that route, let her walk.

Q.26: They said they found body parts in your Refrigerator? Is that the truth?

A.26: Ah Hugh Sure, There's some wild stories around here. You think that's going to make me pay. That's why I'm not paying.

Q.27: Your pretty Smart?

A.27: Yeah, I'm being Upfront laying it all out on the table.

Q.28: Your a religious man aren't you why don't you tell us about the girls chained up in your house?

A.28: That's a trick your trying to play to get me to pay. And your not going to trick me. I'm not paying.

Q.29: What type of religion do you go by?

A.29: Christian.

Q.30: What about the girls, the prostitutes, forget about your wife tell us about them?

A.30: Let her go out and get a job, I'm not talking about that. Your talking stupid.

Q.31: So you did some cabinet work in the kitchen, where did you get the stuff?

A.31: I tiled the floor, I did some cabinet work.

Q.32: Why is your frigidare quality refrigerator?

A.32: Holds up, had it for 3 years . My friends had a Whirlpool and it broke down, wait till the warranty is up you'll see it will break down.

Q.33: Did you put a body in the refrigerator?

A.33: I'm not talking to you if you ask silly questions. I'm not paying that's the matter with her she should go out and get a job.

Q.34: Who should go out and get a job?

A.34: She, my wife she used to work at the Espire Travel Agency 48 or 50th its on parkside Ave. She's filing a petition for support.

> Q.35: When was the last time you talked to your wife?
>
> A.35 In court, You's guys got the petition that says all of that.
>
> Q.36: What about these girls that were chained up in your house?
>
> A.36: Do you think it will rain?
>
> Statement ended.
>
> (signed)
>
> P/O R.A. Young #5735 SCU-1-D
>
> 6:40AM 03-25-87
>
> Cpl. G. Withers #8204 SCU-1
>
> (Refused to Sign)

Heidnik learned to use craziness and memory lapses as a convenience. He learned to *play it crazy*. He knew how insane he really was; only he knew that the fantasies and delusions were being played over and over again. Eventually, Heidnik became a professional at being mentally ill. He collected benefits from the Veterans Administration and from Social Security. At times, he would lose control to his dreams and they increased. He would talk to no one about these dreams. He met only the societal expectations of "crazy."

When Heidnik was lost in his dreams he became mute. Talking interrupted his delusional dream. These were the times he talked of god and "cookies in his throat." These kinds of things were humorous to Heidnik and fit the norm of crazy. Heidnik is absolutely correct in his assessment. *He is crazy, not*

stupid. The problem is that he does not realize how insane he is. The insanity is inside, in his delusions, the things he never talks about. The insanity is not in the outward crazy acts. As a fantasy driven serial killer he is not insane as insanity is expected to be, his insanity is being driven to fulfill his fantasy world, the insanity becomes apparent only after the internal world is acted out.

Heidnik actually learned to manipulate as a youth. He was able to manipulate his internal world to bring him pleasure. He became an expert at manipulating his fantasies. This was done through long periods of time in isolation, such as standing in the corner silently for hours at a time after being punished. He became an expert at internal manipulation because he had no power or *control* over his external world.

Internally, he was able to control his self-image through his beliefs in his delusions. In the external world, he was degraded by the other kids as an oddity and by the embarrassment to his father. Heidnik learned that he was what his fantasy made him.

Gary Heidnik can only function in a structured setting. This structured environment must also include a repetitive setting for long periods of time. It must be remembered that there is no Gary Heidnik, only what his fantasies tell him he is truly exists. His internal world dictates what he is for any specific period of time. Thus he can have success for a short period of time in such a structured setting. Once the structure ends, he falls apart.

The structured settings where Gary Heidnik had his initial successes were as follows:
- Military School
- U.S. Army
- Practical Nurse
- University of Pennsylvania
- Church of the United Ministers of God
- Mental Institutions
- Western Penitentiary, Pittsburgh

In addition, there was a success of Gary Heidnik that was reported by the news media with great interest after his arrest and during his trial. This was Heidnik's status as a financial genius. It was reported in the Philadelphia press that Heidnik's stock portfolio was between $500,000 and $600,000. When asked why he took the case, Heidnik's brilliant defense lawyer, A. Charles Peruto Jr. gave one of his favorite one liners, "I have 100,000 good reasons."

Often times in psychiatric interviews, Heidnik would be asked about these investment strategies. In my interviews with Heidnik, he also discussed his money and his investments. As was mentioned before, and as can be seen by a careful review of his records, Heidnik often stated that his stock information came from god or Jesus. He says he has no memory of that, and denies it emphatically. He admits to talking to god about other things but not about stocks.

This credibility gap was discussed with Heidnik. He either actually does not remember telling the doctors this, or he has been caught in a lie. I choose to believe that he does not actually remember it. He was in a highly stressful suicidal state each time he told the doctors about god and the stock tips. Here is an excerpt from a letter written to me by Heidnik from prison:

> As to your point of god giving me stock tips and having told all these doctors that; well I don't remember telling them that. Yes god does talk to me and gives me good advice but none of it on the stock market.
>
> If god had given me advice I'd probably have done a lot better. Although I've done well in the market my success is over rated. I'm much better at saving money than investing it. Consider for

instance when I got incarcerated in 1979 for a misdemeanor. I was in jail for felonies and the social security and V.A. had to keep paying me in full my pensions for the 5 years I was locked up. Wasn't that in the parole records or mentioned by the PRC or Doctor Bora? They knew about it. You better BELIEVE THEY KNEW ABOUT IT. They had an inside track on every penny that came into that institution or went out. I'm pretty sure they all read all of my mail and they knew all my moves in the stock market. Dr. Bora occasionally mentioned in general terms my investments. Didn't they mention that in my parole request? If they didn't that shows deceit on their part. But more on that later. The point is that I was receiving about $20,000 a year while in jail and I spent very little of it on myself. I donated it almost entirely to the church. So figure an average donation of $15,000 to $20,000 a year, for five years and you get about $85,000 or $90,000. I started off with about $115,000 to $125,000 in the church in 1979 so that gives you about $200,000 from other sources. When I left the church in 1983 it was worth about $350,000 to $400,000. That means I made for the church through good investing about $150,000 over a five year period. That's not bad but it's not as spectacular as the media claims. What did they claim anyways? Something like $15,000 into a half a million. It was as much good savings habit as good investments. Some of my buys were 18 3/4% Philadelphia Electric bonds at 100% per. When you buy something that pays about 20% a year just how much cogitation is there? I'm a little vain and enjoy being considered a financial genius but I'm really only average. God didn't give me any pointers either or the results would have been really spectacular. *It puzzles me too this unconcern on*

god's part for the money was for his church.

Heidnik discussed his study of the stock market with me at some length. In fact, he gave me some tips on writing style after he read drafts of my article intended for the American Psychological Association. He compared my writing to a "dry prunes" and sent me an article by one of his favorite writers, Andrew Tobias. The Tobias article was intended to show me how to improve my writing because if Tobias could make that particular topic interesting then I could make the story of Heidnik a best seller, according to Heidnik.

> Witness how he converts totally mundane topics like federal defecates and taxes into very readable and plausible subjects. He is so persuasive that he makes paying taxes seem like a pleasurable experience.

The Tobias article conspired Heidnik to talk eloquently about Tobias and the stock market.

> You mentioned you found Mr. Andrew Tobias dull and sleep invoking. If you think he is sleep invoking you should read some of the other financial news articles. I find many of them not only dull but impossible. But you have to give Mr. Tobias and others like Adam Smith credit. They have picked a dull topic to write about but they do "at least for me" make it readable and understandable. And talk about dull what could be duller then reading quotations from the New York Stock Market. That's dull. But boy if you got some money invested there it suddenly gets

interesting, exquisitely fascinating in fact. Try it. Buy some stocks and see if you don't wind up pursuing that stocks daily vicissitudes in the market quotations. But more on the financial strategies later.

Heidnik was always extremely protective, and manipulative regarding the topic of his churches assets. In prison, mail is monitored. Heidnik was very conscious of this. His psychiatrist at Graterford, Dr. Bora, was a typical "prison shrink." She was inattentive and did not fully believe, or recognize, his act of psychosis. Whenever he was in one of these active phases Heidnik had to "act out" to get attention. The attention he sought was not to make him the center of events, but to get needed treatment and help. Remember "I'm crazy but not stupid."

Heidnik had seen through the thinly veiled attempts by social service employees at therapy. He had also seen that these psychologists and psychiatrists often get into power struggles to demonstrate who is in command.

> As for Dr. Bora, you are under a misconception of her. I do not regard her in a kindly light and am convinced that she was one of the leaders of the conspiracy against me. I got the distinct impression she was playing mind games with me. About the first week of every month, she called me into her office and cheer me up with the news, 'I think we're going to parole you this month!" That was the upper then at the end of the month she or the PRC would inform me, "nope no parole this month!" this was the downer. Up and down, up and down every month. It was a

variable roller coaster. It was obvious they were trying to exert psychological pressure on me but for what end? I thought part of it was due to having been contacted by a Philadelphia detective, Patrick Devlin he was the one who organized the frame up and put me in jail in the first place.

I was thoroughly convinced that the purpose for lying to me was racially motivated and because I violated the blue code! I also knew that they were all lying to me. When they said I wasn't being paroled to Coatesville because Coatesville had so far refused to accept me, I knew this was pure chimera. I had written not once but several times to the Superintendent of Coatesville and he assured me that I'd be accepted as soon as the parole board contacted him. So that Dr. Bora and the Parole Board were obviously lying. But why? Just how much vengeance did they require of a white man who committed the sin of miscegenation.

It then occurred to me that maybe there was another motive for their lies. Maybe it was money. Perhaps they had designs on the churches assets because they would often discuss openly my stock market maneuvers. So I designed a little experiment. I am fairly certain that the "prison authorities" read all my mail avidly, so I wrote a spurious letter to my daughter who's mother is on the churches board of directors, that I had changed the membership of the board and that many like her mother were no longer on the board. I'm not bragging but this is actually a very

ingenious move on my part. Since the only way they could pilfer the churches resources was to control the church board or by circumventing it entirely the selection of a new and COMPETENT BOARD would block this. Do you know what their response was? When they realized that they could no longer steal that money they paroled me (to Coatesville Mental Hospital) two weeks after the letter, NOT also coincidentally everyone seemed to lose interest in me and they ceased to persecute me. For more than 5 years while incarcerated I thought all the punishment and harassment was racially motivated but now I believe it was mostly money at least by the leaders. Two of these leaders seeking these illicit profits were Detective Patrick Devlin and Dr. Bora. Sally Snaffer was also a ring leader, but her views were different. I believe she was motivated not by money but by the lies of Devlin and Angeanette's family.

This may sound like the common cries of innocence, persecution and frame-ups made by every inmate in prison. And like most, there is some accuracy proved by the record. According to Dr. Bora's notes acceptance to Coatesville was done early. The letter was written by Heidnik to the Superintendent of Coatesville.

Heidnik continued:

My minimum sentence was up and I was unequivocally qualified for parole. I had money, a place to go (Jack Cassidy) no misconducts or disciplinary problems etc. If to be paroled all I had to do was talk why wouldn't I talk?" (Author's

note: Heidnik was mute for nearly 3 years.) Since I was 100% disabled service connected veteran applying to a veteran's hospital for a service connected illness they had to accept me whether I was talking or not. Their only reasons for denying me parole was entirely mercenary. Once that money was removed from their grasps there was no longer any reason for their charade and so they not only paroled me, but everyone lost interest in me.

Looking at the records of imprisonment from 1979 to 1983, it was obvious that Heidnik was mentally ill. Of course, he was no more or less mentally ill then he was in 1962, 1963, 1966, 1967, 1968, 1969, 1971, 1972, 1973, etc. prior to any trouble with the law. But he fell through the cracks in the system. The system had no way of identifying the *emerging ritualistic serial killer.*

Heidnik had to add more and more to prove that his accusations were not simply persecutory delusions similar to that of other inmates.

Now I'm going to play a kind of game with you. I'm not trying to be cute or anything but it seems to be the best way I know of to make a point. If I came right out and said some things you'd think I'm crazy, and I want to appear credible to you. So please don't be mad and don't be impatient.

As you know I've started the church and it had

sizable assets about $125,000 in 1978 and about $350,000 to $400,000 in 1983. So we know there was a lot of money involved. Ok? Suppose, just suppose you were a crook and wanted to steal this money and knew the following information I'm giving you. PLUS all the medical information you already have. You know my medial profile pretty well.

When I started the church there were five people on the Board of Directors. One Evelyn Nelson, two Dorothy McNight, three Maxcine Jones, four Terry Heidnik and five Gary Heidnik.

The churches constitution [Author's note: The constitution is reproduced in its entirety in Appendix 1] said that there should be an election and the winner would be bishop for life. No more elections. The only way a bishop could get put out of office was by dying or resigning. The board members can't even get together and vote the bishop out of office. We held the election and I was elected bishop. In our church the bishop has total control of everything, secular and ecclesiastic. The bishop controls completely all finances and doesn't have to answer to anyone. He doesn't even have to make a financial report to the board even if they were interested. Which they were not. As bishop I made all the investments, expenditures, etc. myself total and life time control. (Even the Supreme Court Justices can't have that kind of security.) Then you find out the churches money is very vulnerable. Other then this guy Heidnik, there is nobody, hardly knows about this church

and all the money involved. There is really nobody but that the Board of Directors now lets take a look at these one at a time.

Evelyn is presently at Ancora State Hospital. She has plenty of mental problems and is abandoned by her family. In 1978 she was still living in Buval Manor in Philadelphia raising my oldest daughter Angelic. She has problems, especially money problems. Later in 1982 and 1983 she was in a boarding home and abandoned by her kids. Angelic was then being raised by her oldest daughter Sonya Lynn, if she didn't know the amount of money involved, (and she didn't) she could be easily manipulated. If someone offered her a certain amount of money to sign a paper, she would sign, FAST!

Dorothy McNight. This is the woman who lived with me for 10 years. She is about 10 years older than me and spent a lot of years at Byeberry before I knew her. Her mind had continued to degenerate so badly that she had trouble going around the corner without getting lost and she'd sign any document you wanted for a pack of cigarettes.

Maxcine Jones. She is in her right mind but publicly disavowed the church and wants nothing to do with it. So she's off the board no problem.

Terry Heidnik is the only problem. He knew how much money is involved and is nobody's fool. To get him to vote your way is going to be tough.

To hold an election for bishop I would of course had to be dead or resign so I don't count. Since Maxcine probably dropped from the board there are only 3 voting members left. Dorothy, Evelyn and Terry, since you only need 2 votes out of 3 Terry doesn't matter. You know or maybe even getting the votes of Dorothy and Evelyn are the only standing between you and all that money is one Gary Bishop.

Now remember don't think like yourself. Think like a crooked cop named Devlin. He wants to steal the money which is so vulnerable, but he'd prefer to do it legally. How would you do it? And keep in mind my medical profile (which Devlin knew also).

Devlin definitely knew of the churches funds but not at first. He didn't know the night they came to arrest me. But I wasn't there so they searched the apartment and left. Angeanette was home at the time. When I got home in the morning I found several statements from Merrill Lynch missing. These statements would have told him how much the church was worth and give him my sock broker's name. Devlin also stole an expensive pocket knife.

My stock broker was Robert Kirkpatrick III from about 1973 to 1987. If they got to Kirkpatrick they could by pass the board. But they'd have to do something about me. Kirkpatrick would sell his mother out. All the funds are at either Merrill Lynch or the Provident Bank on 40th and Chestnut Street. The funds have no protection other then being in these 2 institutions and the funds could only be transferred with my say so and signature, no other but only as long as I remained bishop. My first attorney Donald Levine could not be trusted. I think that Devlin got to him some how and had him working for him. When I realized at the arraignment that he was selling me out I dropped him and hired Robert Pressman (with Jack Bulkin). Mr. Pressman at the beginning fought hard and fair for me. He asked me if I knew why there were people who wanted me so badly? Do I have a lot of money? I told him a little about the church but I didn't think that he believed me.

Neither did any of the psychiatrists who later called Heidnik grandiose, because he told them that he started the church. They also labeled him "delusive and out of touch with reality" when he told them that he was a bishop of the church that he founded. A very healthy church. At times Heidnik is delusional or paranoid, but not when he talks about his church. The staff professionals had missed the point. They missed the crux of his illness and based their diagnoses, therapy and opinions on superficial information gained in text books interviews. The diagnosis came from the *Diagnostic and Statistical Manual of the American Psychiatric Association* [DSM] rather than interpreted data. The need for them to be right

and to place Heidnik into a pat diagnosis is overly evident.

Heidnik of course is guilty. But where are the experts now? They share in the guilt. They failed. Passing a board certification does not prepare one for Gary Heidnik, or any other ritualistic serial killer.

When there were correct evaluations, they were ignored. Only ignorance was left to prove their diagnosis and points of view. The medical records produce a horror story. A trial of tragic incompetence. My favorite sentence from one of these reports is by a psychiatrist at a local mental hospital clinic.

The reports states, "that with continued psychotherapy Mr. Heidnik's prognosis was good." The report was made to the family court so that Gary Heidnik could visit his child. The date of that report was March 18, 1987.

Sandra Lindsay died March 18, 1987, was carved into pieces was cooked, put into a freezer, bones buried and put into a cup, *all by an individual whose prognosis was good.*

CHAPTER 8

SUICIDE AND CONTROL

Suicide attempts are sprinkled all throughout Gary Heidnik's life. *It is manipulation on a grand scale.* Once again, listen to Gary Heidnik in the letter he wrote to me in December of 1988 regarding his suicide attempts of the 5th of February of 1986.

> Again about the suicide. You amazed me there I didn't think you'd see it so clearly. I thought maybe only a medical doctor could see it. But you did spot it. You confirmed more than confirmed my faith in you. You're one of the truly cerebrally enlightened. By looking at my medical records it became obvious that my suicide attempts are very, very predictable. Every time I get into a stressful situation or a lot of pressure is applied I respond by trying to commit suicide. It's almost like a knee jerk reaction. Put pressure and tension on one side and a suicide attempt will come out the other.

Heidnik had learned that by attempting suicide he regained control of any stressful situation that he might find

himself involved. There is a history of suicide in Heidnik's family also. His mother died on Memorial Day from an overdose of hair dye which contained a mercury based substance. Gary Heidnik later developed an allergy to all substances which contain mercury.

Over the course of time he also became an expert on suicide attempts. He studied them. He learned all he could about the collateral effects, and he knew what his chances of survival really were. Heidnik always had something to gain from these attempts, but he often came close to death. Keep in mind that Heidnik doesn't like pain, such as the pain that he anticipates from the electric chair. He does not, to quote him, "relish the though of becoming a french fry."

Heidnik has revealed his research, and his thinking in the several suicide attempts. His letters review his planning and his control over the situations. By suicide, or the attempt, Heidnik always regained control of the situation.

> As you may know after so many failed suicide attempts on my part I facetiously label myself an expert on the subject. One of my most inspired attempts occurred in January 1979. There is some equivocation about this attempt but let me assure you I was sincere. I had read a book by Robin someone or another (I forget his last name) called Tales of the Green Berets. He wrote that the North Vietnamese sometimes put slivers of bamboo in American food which ingested cause unstoppable internal hemorrhage. Think about it. It's plausible right? Also in a movie something like "The Monster Who Roamed The West" the villain crushed a glass figurine and put it in the victims food. This petutitively caused fatal hemorrhaging. This also seemed plausible to me. So upon

spending my first night in Graterford I determined to commit suicide and I incorporated this data into my plot. I unscrewed the light bulb, broke it, crushed some of the glass in my metal cup and tried to swallow it. It wouldn't go down however with mixing some water on a spoon it did go down. Sort of a consummate paranoidal if you will.

The contention that you could surreptitiously poison someone with ground glass is fallacious, since it is readily detectable. But you could do it with their convenience. So having ingested this delicacy I layed down to await the results. After a couple of hours I awoke with an over powering sensation of nausea and groped to the sink where I vomited a mass of black viscosity, digested blood. This event assured me of my success of my endeavors and I again reclined with a sense of ecstasy of my impending demise. Unfortunately I woke that morning completely viable suffering no ill effects. My postulation is that when I vomited the blood I evacuated all the ground glass. Hence no more irritation, no more bleeding. Since the x-rays showed no glass residue there was a assumption of mendacity. I assure that there was no mendacity the effort was sincere or be it unique. One of the greatest fictions pertaining to suicide is the slashing of one's wrists. Theoretically this is possible but I know of no incidents of success. Only in fiction does self induced mutilation succeed. There are many people who have tried this though but they are still walking around. None is in the grave yard. Someone you know has tried it. Guess who? My wife Betty that's

who she slashed her left wrist seventeen times in a very determined effort, but failed. That's why you always see her in long sleeves, she is ashamed of the success. Don't mention that I told this to you, in confidence. At any rate slashed wrists is just another one of the fictions of modern life.

After this alleged suicide attempt, his attorney Jack Bulkin successfully petitioned the court to remove Heidnik from the main population to the psychiatric ward. Heidnik had completed another successful manipulation.

The next suicide attempt that Heidnik discussed were the inquiries into his February 5, 1986 attempt were he ingested between 7.8 and 9 grams of thorozine, a quantity of gin and sat in an enclosed garage in a truck with the motor running. Tony Brown, Heidnik's gopher, was also mentally retarded and found him. Heidnik describes Brown as :

> Tony although capable of reading and writing and driving a car has trouble getting his facts straight. He is absolutely terrified of policemen and as such told the cops anything he thought they wanted to hear. That's how he got arrested.

Tony confessed to two counts of murder when arrested. Later, after interviews with the hostages, the charges were dropped. It would seem that Heidnik's evaluation of Tony Brown was pretty good. But Tony Brown was competent enough to find Heidnik unconscious, and in a comatose state in the garage, and rushed him to nearby Temple University Hospital. It was according to these hospital records, that we know that Heidnik was comatose. He needed to be intubated orally, and placed on an ventilator for 36 hours. He had "dolls eyes" which are described as "unresponsive," as if starring into

another dimension.

Heidnik was given Nacan which is considered a super anti-drug to restore vital signs. He had an irregular heart beat. Heidnik says he has little or no memory of the events surrounding this attempt. It is important the tone and quality of his questions, and identify who is the *dominant character* in his personality, and who is doing the questioning. *It certainly appears as if the manipulator was making an academic question out of a suicide attempt.* But part of Bishop Gary filters through in the second part of his words, which was only days later. The treatise he was referring to is an article I wrote on serial murders.

> In your treatise you made some reference to my suicide attempts of February 1986. This event has always been something of an enigma to me since I had been unconscious for three days. The last thing I remember was seeing Tony opening the garage door and had just enough strength to lock the van door before becoming insensate. Could you fill me in on the blank spots? For instance: How long was I unconscious? You mentioned I was intubated; what and how many tubes? You also mentioned respiratory assistance was that simply nasal 0/2 or perhaps ventilation? Did they at anytime administer CPR? Here's my biggest conundrum. It seems to me that the doses of carbon monoxide, thorozine and alcohol should have been fatal. Why wasn't it? Did they possibly administer some super anti-drug like Nercon (I'm not sure if I spelled that name properly). I only remember waking up about 3 days later and signing AMA. I have no recollections of even going home or how I got home. I doubt if your records can help there.

I had over $800 on me before they arrested me. When I got home my wallet was empty. Any mention of that money?"

Later I was to find that Heidnik's questions, *and my answers*, were used to manipulate and control again. Heidnik was not unconscious for 3 days. He was ventilated for only 24 hours. Also, he did not remember the $800, which is not in keeping with his well developed image of being able to track money. Not only did he sign himself out of the hospital against medical advice, he did so with a diagnosis of pneumonia as well. He was weak and only off the respirator for one day when he signed himself out of the hospital. *What is important is not that this was his 12th suicide attempt, but that this attempt almost succeeded.* The doctors at Temple decided not to keep him against his will because he convinced them that he "won't try again." He told them that this was just an attempt following a fight with his wife. He told them he had pressing business at home, and he had to look after his house and his personal accessories. They let him go. He walked out again. He was discharged in a weakened state, with a prescription for antibiotics and thorozine. *But only 3 days before he had ingested 100-100 milligram tablets or 9.8 grams.* Manipulation and malingering was allowed by the hospital. If they had committed him could the murderers have been prevented? At that point Heidnik had been hospitalized at least 21 times. He had a criminal record. He had been in Fairview Hospital for the Criminally Insane twice. Who is malingering? Who is really in control? Once again read Heidnik's words:

Several times he subtlety mentioned the word malingerer. This suicide attempt was a part of that. Does this attempt sound in any way insincere? The last time I heard suicide is a manifestation of mental illness. Also as of November 1986 I would

have been considered a permanent disability since I have been classified disabled for 20 years and could not be cut. My pension was not even remotely threatened so how or why would I stage the suicide attempt if I wasn't sincere? Tony's arrival and interference was quite unexpected. He was out and I figured he'd be out all day and even if he wasn't he had no business going into the garage. If Barbara hadn't told him where I was and if he didn't get nosey I'd have succeeded. Even after he found me and I locked the door to the van he told me he wasn't sure what to do but after waiting 15 minutes or so he called the Rescue Ambulance. He was proud of having saved me but I berated him for doing it and even made him promise not to do it in the future. He promised he wouldn't.

This part of Heidnik's recollections are verified in the extensive medical records. Now follow Heidnik through his recollections of his last suicide attempt.

Another suicide attempt I made in jail, that's the one that made the papers. You don't think I was malingering do you? Even the prison was convinced of my sincerity and they're some of the biggest skeptics around. I almost succeed in hanging myself in the shower. I tried 4 different times in my cell but I couldn't get enough height. There is a bar on the desk in my cell but it was only 3 feet high. There was something magical in that shirt I was using. I used it in the shower and it worked there too. I told the guard I was taking it

in the shower to wash. But for some reason he got suspicious and peaked into the shower and saw me hanging there. In getting me off he even cut my head on the shower head but I didn't feel any pain since I was unconscious. He took me out and laid me on the floor and gave me oxygen. I was out for several more minutes before coming to. Then they took me to a hospital for observations and tests. The officer's name who caught me was Officer Love. They reprimanded him severely for not catching me sooner. Yes, they reprimanded him not praised him. Later he even asked me how it felt to be dead.

Hanging is an interesting phenomena and I can describe it as someone who has experienced it, like no one else can. The perception that you strangle and slowly asphyxiate isn't necessarily slow, I could never hang myself that way. In my case when using that particular T-shirt, and only that T-shirt, I experienced complete and sudden and total unconsciousness. There was no straggling or gasping for breath. I believe that the T-shirt was able to cut off the blood to my brain and that's what caused the blackness not the lost of breath. Also there's no pain. I'd give it 4 stars as a means for committing suicide so long as you do it so it cuts off the blood supply, and not the breathing. Loss of breath is too much suffering.

The facts about Heidnik's "4-star" suicide attempts support much of what he talked about in our conversations. He had intermittent redness of the entire neck, and laceration of the back of the head. They placed him on suicide watch, and as he was unable to eat, he was placed on intravenous. He was discharged on April 3, 1987 to the psychiatric hospital at Grater-

ford prison. The x-rays showed no broken bones or disturbed air passages. Yet he did not use a hangman's noose; he rather, used his own T-shirt which could cut the blood flow and/or air flow and cause unconsciousness.

At his murder trial in June 1988, the guard, Mr. Love, stated clearly that Heidnik was unconscious and he thought he was dead. He in fact, stopped and attempted to revise him and when that didn't wake him, they got oxygen. The malingerer was once again in control. The malingerer was not Heidnik the man who attempted the suicide, but the man who regained control when the attempt failed.

I once questioned Heidnik as to what he thought was his most accomplished suicide attempt particularly because of the malingering charges made at his trial. Heidnik became quite descriptive.

> I should recommend the ways of suicide the absolute best, most preferred way is the way I did it in 1986. I took about 4,000 milligrams of thorozine with about 16 oz. of gin. That combination of alcohol and drugs is reputed to be very lethal. The alcohol though gets you so high that you are actually enjoying yourself and having a good time. I had the truck running and filling up the garage with carbon monoxide but I think the effects of that were minimal or non existent since it hadn't been long enough. As a matter of fact it was counter productive since the sounds of the running truck attracted Tony to the garage. By the way, I did achieve a little fame and notoriety for the hanging attempt at D.C. [District Court Detention Center] After that they completely changed all the shower heads so that no one could do it again, ha-ha-ha.

Probing the Mind of a Serial Killer   J.A. Apsche

Heidnik is not an malingerer but he is an *expert manipulator*. On New Year's day, January 1, 1989, Gary Heidnik attempted suicide one more time. Inside his cell at the maximum security prison, Heidnik had stock-piled Thorozine. After completing a 28 page letter to me, he took the Thorozine at 3 A.M. He was found unconscious by a guard and rushed to the hospital. It is important to note that this suicide attempt followed his in-depth questions to me regarding his suicide attempt of February 1986. He again used the Thorozine but without the gin and the carbon monoxide. It seems a certainty to me that he knew he would not die. He knew when the guards would check him on death row. He knew he would be removed from the prison and sent to the hospital. He knew how to regain *control* of himself, the prison, the media and all his surrounding circumstances.

CHAPTER 9

INTIMACY, BONDING AND CONTROL

When interviewed by a psychiatrist in 1984 Heidnik was found to have persecutory grandiose delusions, disoriented insight, severely impaired judgment and was determined to be incompetent. The psychiatrist predicted that either Heidnik would commit heinous crimes in the future or he would hurt himself.

One area common to all serial killers is an internal battle between intimacy [closeness] and control. In some cases, it appears that there has never been any intimacy in their lives, but a substitution of control for closeness. The result is that they learn to relate to others in the only way they know, without intimacy and with control. The inadequacy comes from severe rejection, perceived rejection or emasculation by one or both parents. Ressler's 1988 study showed that 21 of the 36 subjects studied lived in households dominated by the mother.

The study further stated that there was a noninvolvment with the father in the families that had remained intact. They reported a "psychological and social disengagement" was experienced by the boy. When this compounded an already ambivalent relationship with the mother, early signs of negative

human attachment or disregarding potentially positive ones have been expected. The abuse can be so severe, that abuse actually becomes the model for how they control their own lives. They have no ability to relate and no capacity for intimacy. Their relationships are defined only by their ability to control, or not control, others.

Perhaps the most interesting result was that most offenders said that they did not have a satisfactory relationship with the father and that the relationship with the mother was highly ambivalent in emotional quality. Sixteen of the men reported cold or uncaring relationships with their mothers, and twenty-six reported similar relationships with their fathers." [pg. 22]

Their feelings of inadequacy are such that even if outward appearances of masculinity have them seen as being in control, inside they are in torment and in constant severe pain. They are abusive because they cannot control in any other way. The people they victimize are people they have found a way to control. They may have sub-normal IQs, be drug or alcohol addicts, or they may simply be controlled through force and fear.

Intimacy may appear to be a vague and undefinable feeling. Yet it can have several specific behavioral characteristics. Amidon, et.al. in 1992 published a book called *The Intimacy Manual.*. This book details the patterns of intimacy and control in a general way. A detailed excerpt from the book are given as Appendix 2. The decades of research that lead to that book have shown that people often confuse intimacy and control issues. Dr. Amidon, in his work with normal individuals, has shown that people will substitute control when intimacy needs are unmet or uncontrollable. Individuals that have never experienced intimacy, or bonding, can only respond with control.

Richard Rappaport has written that the sexual sadist is in

need of taking control or demonstrating his power. He sees that the actual murder itself becomes a form of intimacy between the killer and the victim.

In the book *Mass Murder: America's Growing Menace*, Levine and Fox state that the pleasure and exhilaration that serial killers derive from repeated murder is the absolute control over other human beings. They quote Ted Bundy: "A rape wasn't really the important part, it was the dominance."

Thus the need for intimacy is eventually released in the form of total control by the actual death of the victim. In cases where there have been necrophilia and cannibalism, we have an extension of that ultimate control which can continue long after the "murderous orgasm." Harrison Marty Graham possessed 7 bodies, even until parts rotted off, in order to retain control. As Graham said: "they were mine and weren't going no where."

Gary Heidnik retained control over the murdered Sandra Lindsay by cooking her body parts together with dog food and rice and feeding the concoction to his other victims. Thus she remained captive in the digestive tract of people whom he controlled, and by extension he still controlled her even after death.

The conflict of a sexual serial killer like Heidnik centers on intimacy and control needs. His intimacy needs were never met, and he substituted control or power. The following diagram attempts to simplify the intimacy control continuum . The move from inanimate objects such as pornography into masturbatory\ fantasies may be determined by the power of the sexual drive and conflict with the guilt that it cannot be controlled. Religion may be used to help suppress the drive or fantasy. Heidnik used good deeds, preaching to the retarded, taking them to dinner, taking them on trips, etc. Sometimes the religion makes the fantasy more intense. A "pagan" quality is attached to the delusional fantasy. This is often been mistaken as "Satanism." The ritual or belief, or paganism is born

in the killers fantasy. They become as powerful as God; they have the power over life and death. This is often not a conscious decision to become god-like but a taste for blood and a regression into a primal state. All inhibitions, religious morals, social rules and laws are broken in order to fulfill the delusional fantasy. The fantasy begins in childhood and allows endless rehearsals prior to an actual murder. Because of these rehearsals it is almost impossible to catch these people before enormous horror and damage occur. The higher the intelligence, and the more in touch with his instinctual primitive drive, the more unlikely a capture is. The Green River killer has murdered over 125 people and is yet unknown. Randy Kraft was accused of killing well over 100 people in three states, yet there is evidence of only one kill. The task may seem impossible unless it is remembered that the only motive is in the fantasy and that is where to look for clues.

INTIMACY	CONTROL
Emotionally absent parent(s)	Mental & emotional abuse
Sexual & physical abuse	Internal deviant fantasy world/ deviant sexual fantasy
Puberty	Masturbatory fantasy Instinctual drive for self-gratification Pornography
Torture / murder	Control drives the fantasy
Necrophilia	Slaves and control
Cannibalism	Dismemberment

As previously mentioned I'd written a paper on serial killers based on a review of scientific research, interviews and FBI crime statistics. I gave it to Heidnik to read and for his comments. Interestingly, many of his comments were accurate and

have stimulated me to further research and, of course, more questions. Yet on the point of a child's need for bonding and closeness something in the paper stimulated Heidnik to an emotional and detailed response.

Once more, listen to the clear response from John Wesley Dodd during his PBS *Frontline* interview:

> I don't know if I have any feelings, maybe that's my birth defect. I wasn't ever — I wasn't even born with feelings. I don't know because I never felt anything about anything.

The need for bonding is apparent in all human beings. Psychological research has clearly demonstrated that children from homes of abuse are more likely to abuse. It is also true of closeness. If children are from homes where there is little or no intimacy, then they will most likely never know how to achieve intimacy in their adult lives, unless they are subsequently taught.

In fact, research on incest survivors indicates that children who were physically and sexually abused, may equate pain with what they had learned was closeness. Closeness or bonding is an instinctual need. When a human being does not receive bonding in the infant stages, it appears to remain a basic human need that may never be fulfilled.

Because of this need for intimacy, and because such individuals have never experience closeness, they often substitute control for closeness. This continued, unfulfilled need for bonding may manifest itself in a variety of behaviors. Some may seek an endless string of sexual partners, achieving sex, but no intimacy. Others may seek even more extreme sexual exploration. Although sexual exploration between two consenting adults is healthy, as long as it remains mutually agreeable, when it leads to perversion, severe sadomasochistic behavior, child pornography and other such exploitation and

misuse, it is not normal or healthy. When it leads to delusional fantasies and acting out behavior(s) that inflict pain on others, it is severely aberrant behavior in need of treatment.

When, in children, control is substituted for intimacy [as manipulation and control substituted for closeness], the child mistakenly learns that control is a *substitute* for intimacy. For the sexual sadist, there is a need to take control to demonstrate power and virility. *The mode of death selected is one which indicates that the victim had meaning for the killer, and that the intimacy in the murderous act is part of the close bond between the murderer and the victim formed in the killers fantasies and delusions.*

Now listen to Heidnik

> As everybody knows, as much as America would like to think of itself as a homogeneous society it is not. America used to call itself the melting pot but no more. America is a complex social group consisting of many other social groups. The most dominant social group is the infamous WASPS of which by birth I am dutifully a member but of which we both know I am in reality an outcast of. Having being exiled and ostracized by my own social group was I condemned to live a life in limbo a virtual hermit or would I...? Would I what?
>
> As we both know I am plagued with mental problems but I am not incompetent. This is a condition that can be summarized in the little homily "he's crazy but not stupid." So to satisfy this need for belonging (as you phrased it of bonding) I began to cast about looking for another social group to join. Since it was virtually impossible to join another group as a respected equal, the only

way I could join was by ingratiating myself to them. The word ingratiating is properly used there since there could never be true acceptance. After many trials and disappointments I achieved moderately success with some of the other fringes of black society. As I say though it wasn't true acceptance, and to belong I continually had to pay my dues. I did however achieve a measure of bonding with the companionship with an old mentally ill black woman. This junction however produced a bonding at only an emotional level, there was virtually no intellectual communication and perhaps to societies gratification it produced no off-spring. So we weren't interfered with and the union was preserved for about 10 years. I had of course desired children desperately and since I couldn't have any with Dorothy I began looking else where. That was when I chanced upon lower societies fellow rejects, Angeanette Davidson. She had been rejected and unloved by her own social group as well as her family, as I had been. We both experienced this ostracism, this vacuum of belonging. Two ships cast a drift in the night, searching and by luck we found each other. Perhaps because our needs were so great, it is that our love was so strong. We also shared a common desire to have children. Unfortunately for us though we were of different races she black and me white.

Where as Dorothy and I couldn't have any children the bigots begrudgingly left us alone. But now with Angeanette children were not only possible but one had arrived and more were in the offering. This was a situation racists couldn't

permit to endure. So they undertook to separate Angeanette and myself. Because of my mental illness and Angeanette's functional retardation they resorted to the fact that I was crazy and taking advantage of the helpless. They succeeded in framing me for a crime that never occurred and putting me in jail for 5 years. Upon being released I sought to rejoin that social group which had given me the greatest measure of acceptance ... the mentally handicapped. The mentally handicap do indeed form their own social group and it isn't influenced by things like race. Most handicapped are rejected by so called normal society and seek comfort and belonging with each other. Indeed this social group's pride even built my church. It was a territory no main line church was interested in since it was both poor and took a great measure of patience and time. Understanding if you will. By the handicapped I was readily accepted. I was compatible in two ways. Since I was also mentally ill they recognized me as one of their own.

Also since I was extremely competent and willing to assist I was doubly acceptable. It was a synchronic relationship, I exchanged my competence for their companionship and friendship. Pre pro quo if you will I never took advantage of anyone or exploited anyone. If I had they would have quickly rejected me and abandoned me. As for fiduciary relationships the money usually went from me to them. I was always buying them food in restaurants, coffees, brunch etc. Especially to members of my church. As you know I often took them to Roy Rogers, or to

MacDonalds, Great Adventure, Hershey Park etc. One of their favorite paddings was a smorgasbord called Duffys...at various times I was called upon to supply room and board and if they had money I charged them $200 a month, if they didn't have it I supplied it gratis.

If you think you can make a profit today on $200 a month try it. That's why everybody always charges more for room and board. They even had their own private rooms, T.V.'s, stereo and the use of the house. Barbara Johnson got the use of the master bedroom or water bed etc. I slept in the back bedroom the smallest of them. At one time or another Tony Brown, Gal Lincoln, Robert Johnson roomed with me. There was no financial exploitation on my part. If there was they'd have left along time before they did. They all showed substantial weight gains too since the food was also adequate.

My favorite time was with Sandy [Sandra Lindsay]. My financial rewards for these services were negligible the human rewards were tremendous. I not only achieved a glorified feeling from helping my fellow man but I achieved an almost around the clock companionship and sense of belonging. Still there was a vacuum in my life. I needed bonding and closeness of a wife and children. To achieve this I reached to a even different social group and made one of the biggest mistakes of my life. Falsely that oriental women would be the greatest wives ever in existence, I married a Philippian. I probably arrived at this

conclusion by watching too many Suzy Wong reruns. As a social group maybe Chinese or Japanese make great wives. Filipino women are another story. You've encountered some of these difficulties I believe since you actually came into contact with Betty. If you need more proof just ask Peruto. You and I can both commemorate with him. Anyway my union with Betty was partially successful. It produced a healthy active bouncing son, Jessie. However it also produced a great mental anguish and supplied none of the companionship or bonding I needed so much. It was so hectic that at one point she had me incarcerated for a villainous rape charge and at another point I locked myself in the garage and tried to commit suicide, and even to another point I had myself committed to Coatesville trying to escape her.

As you know my marriage had deteriorated and my relations with the handicapped desegregated. Again I was alone. What to do? What I did you already know. As for the reasons, one very possible I will discuss later, but a unique way of looking at what I did in disturbed state of mind was to create my own social group, or family if you wish. It was a social group in which I was the only male, the only economic provider, the patriarch so to speak, and which was available to me 24 hours a day. Perhaps my needs were best summarized in four words by Rivera, a psychologist in her own right when she said, "you're lonely aren't you?" Having correctly analyzed the situation she then properly exploited my need for bonding to achieve her freedom.

Since the situation was actually repugnant to me I had no such compelling need to be loved, it wasn't actually a difficult deception for her. The rest of the story you know. What is pertinent here is perspective. Since I couldn't achieve a sense of belonging to any other existing social groups in American society I endeavored to create my own social group. One that had to provide the things that I needed love, bonding, children, companionship, etc. For instance any time I felt the need to talk they were there. Where could they go? And they had to listen. Does my explanation seem valid? What as a scientist is your input?

My input was more questions. Questions that invoked difficult responses. It seemed to me that it might have been proven that Josephine Rivera was a co-conspirator. A source told me that the District Attorney's office still get calls from Rivera for money. She had been paid by them to testify. Once again she is alleged to have been involved with the law, on charges of drug abuse and prostitution. During the incidents in Heidnik's basement, Rivera could have left any time she wanted, this was related to me by Lisa Thomas. She also said that Rivera had beat her excessively when Heidnik wasn't there. She told me that on the day that Debra Dudley was murdered, Rivera and Heidnik were both involved in the electrocution. According to Thomas, "...the tricks she taught Gary Heidnik were the same she [Rivera] had learned from her pimp, Fuzzy."

According to Heidnik, Rivera had manipulated the master manipulator, Gary Heidnik. She had initiated some of the harsh punishments, and Lisa Thomas said that she had actually put the electric wires on Debra Dudley. Rivera was paid by the D.A. to testify. She did not call the police willingly on Gary Heidnik, Fuzzy dialed the phone, and forced her to turn him

in.

Much of the evidence regarding Josephina Rivera was suppressed at the trial. Evidence that should have been revealed was not disclosed to the judge during the trial. Anyway, Heidnik was guilty. But beyond that the results of the trial has left Rivera still free to this day —without any treatment. Has another person fallen through the cracks in the system? It is important to review Heidnik's words on what happened in that basement. Heidnik doesn't call what happened murders, he calls them "deaths", "accidents."

> There are several questions regarding the two deaths I was convicted of that I wish to address now. I've already addressed the question of intent. There certainly was no intent on my or Rivera's part to kill either woman, and I think I've already made that partially clear in other letters. For some reason Peurto never properly addressed the issue of intent possibly because he could sell more copies of his book if I got the death sentence.

> Another aspect of their deaths is the technical aspect. Look at the drawings I made. From purely the technical aspect neither death seems possible hence my bemusement. Let's first consider Sandy's death. Everybody has been saying I "hung" her by her arms from the ceiling. The use of the word "hung" or hang is entirely inaccurate. Sandy was not only NOT hung from the ceiling she had both feet solidly on the ground and her arm was at a right angle not even fully extended like so, and this is easy to prove. Nobody has to take my word or even ask the other women.

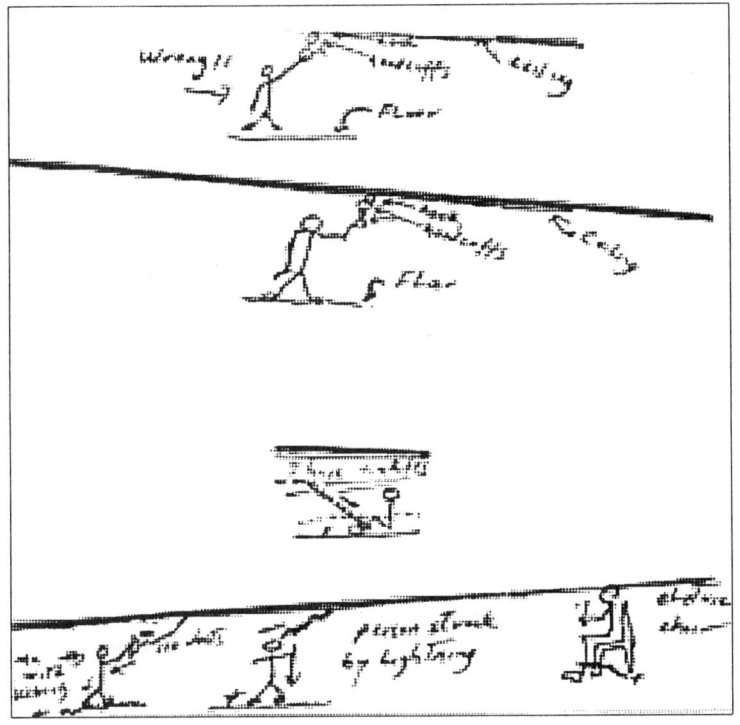

The ceiling (cellar rafters) they are about 6 feet from the floor and the eye bolt or hook or whatever it's called was screwed into the bottom of the rafters, not the sides or anywhere else. Check the holes. Sandy was what about 5 foot 5 inches tall. Now figure the bottom of the eye bolt is about a inch from the ceiling (or rafters) the handcuffs add another 6 inches. So if Sandy's arm (wrist) wasn't 6 feet high but more like 5 foot 5 inches from the floor. These are only estimates, but can easily be checked with a ruler. Anyway this shows definitely that she wasn't hanged from the ceiling

as the news media claims but of course they're not interested in being accurate only in selling papers. Both her feet were on the ground she simply was forced to stand up. She couldn't sit down. If standing is dangerous or fatal there'd be a lot of dead waitresses or sales clerks.

Also she wasn't standing that long that particular time. An hour and a half to be exact. She spent the whole previous night standing up about 12 hours without ill effects. I had let her down that morning and she'd been lying and sitting all that day. I don't know exactly what day it was but it was in February. A movie with Linda Lavin in Australia started up about 8 or 9 o'clock and that is when I stood her up. After about an hour and a half the movie wasn't yet over it broke for a commercial, I went downstairs to check on everyone and Sandy was handing by her arms her legs bent and her head rolled to one side. At first I though she was faking when I realized that she was really dead I was the most shocked of all. How the hell can standing up for an hour and a half be fatal?

The coroner never answered this question and Peruto didn't ask. The coroner stated he didn't know the exact cause of death, but he said he concluded it was murder since the body had been mutilated. Now what kind of conclusion is that? It's not proof and it's certainly not scientific. He didn't know why Sandy died any more than I did. Of course Peruto didn't pursue this issue either. For all anyone knows she may have died of a

stroke or a heart attack or maybe an infection or a fever. Nobody knows. But standing on your feet for an hour and a half is not and never has been fatal. I've asked about this cause of death and got no concrete answer. One answer was maybe it was a broken heart. If they could I'd have been dead long ago and 50 times over with all the pain and punishment I've been through.

Then there's the unthinkable that maybe one of the other girls killed her. This is really a very remote possibility but when dealing with the unknown everything is possible. This theory gains some credence when you realize that Sandy was a lesbian. At one time I even ordered Debbie to appease Sandy's advertent desires. It is entirely possible that one of these women was so repelled by this that they eliminated Sandy rather than see such things continue.

Debra Dudley's death, from a purely technical view point also remains an enigma. They claim she dies of electrocution, but I claim such a decision is inchoate. Here is some of the reasoning for this disclaimer as a child, working with my father wiring houses, I received not one but several electrical shocks while grounded in water. Let me assure you that they were not pleasant but likewise they were not fatal. Because I know from personal experience that electrical shock received while grounded in water are not always habitually fatal.

Another factor about fatal electrical shocks is that they pass through the heart region. When someone is hit by a lightning bolt it strikes them on the head or arms and passes through his heart to where his feet touch the ground he will usually die. Executioners are extremely cognoscente of this phenomena and when electrocuting someone the charges is usually applied at the prisoners head and exits the ankles where another electrode is attached. There by passing through the heart and deadly. They also use a much greater wattage. So consider that as a child the electricity entered through my arm and passes out my feet. Like so (refer to the diagram) you can see in the drawings the electrical charge passes through the heart region but it is only fatal in the later two cases which carries as much wattage. It wasn't fatal to me even though it passed through my heart.

Now consider Debbie when Rivera shocked her she was underground and the charge wasn't applied directly to Debbie but through her chains. Those chains in turn were connected to Debbie's ankles and the ankles were grounded in water. Plus the charge would have entered at the ankles and exited at the ankles where the water made contact. Yet at no time did the charge pass through the heart region. What makes this situation even more puzzling is that the charge is applied to the chain not directly to Debbie plus it had to pass through several feet of steel first. Steel, although not a good conductor of electricity will none the less conduct it, but it would have acted

somewhat as a resistor thus considerably reducing the 110 volts.

The claims of the coroner that Debbie suffered electrical burns on her ankles is inaccurate. Not only Debbie, but Agnes (Donna) and maybe Lisa (I'm not sure about Lisa) had open sores on their ankles caused by chaffing from the muscle clamps. It was those sores on Debbie's ankles that the coroner ascribes to as burns and were not caused by electricity. As ignorant as this coroner is it's amazing that he passed high school science, let alone college. He certainly doesn't understand science or the scientific method. One thing the coroner is good at is though he is a good sycophant for the prosecution.

It goes without saying that when Rivera shocked Debbie she had no intentions of killing her, and neither did I. So to call Debbie's death murder is a miscarriage of terminology since there was no intent to kill. Not only was there no intent but if you consider the technical factors I presented there is also cause to doubt the means of her death. If she didn't die from electrocution, what did kill her? Another broken heart? I doubt it. Her cause of death is just as equivocal as Sandy's.

Also speaking of Rivera, Rivera is not the hero that everyone believes or even a Miss Goody

Goody. Rivera's prime interest in life is her own self interest, and pursuit of a drug habit. She is addicted to Cocaine injections and needs several injections every day. That's why she always wears long sleeve blouses, to conceal the marks in her arms. She's possessed of considerable "street smarts" and does quite well on the street. Once I released her she had ample opportunities to call the police, to run away, and yes even to drive away. The very first night I put her behind the drivers wheel of my car while walking around to the passenger side, she could have easily locked the doors and drove away or run over me first then drive away. As the public health clinic, when the doctor took her for examining in private, she could have run away or asked the doctor for help. She didn't. When we were in McDonalds, Roy Rogers, Dennys, Ponderosa and other restaurants she could have called for help or run away. She didn't.

When I went to the V.A. at Broad and Cherry to arrange a dental appointment, I couldn't find a parking space so I instructed her to drive around the block till I got done. The appointment took more then an hour and she could have easily driven to the nearest police station. She didn't. She had almost total access to the phone in the kitchen and could have gone into the kitchen at anytime, especially when I was asleep and called the police. She didn't. She even set up her friend Vicky for the final kidnapping. Why you ask? Why didn't she ask for help sooner and why set up her colleague?

The answer is explained by her boyfriend. He went public that Rivera tried to get him to rob me with a hammer. When he refused, she didn't want to return so then she called the police. Rivera knew I was carrying $2,000 on my person and she was determined to get it before she turned me in. And if I happened to get killed in the robbery attempt, I feel sorry for her boyfriend since Rivera would have naturally blamed it all on him claiming it was his idea. That's how "street smarts" work and how one feed a drug habit in the ghetto.

There were actually three deaths at 3520 North Marshall not two. When Sandy died she was about two months pregnant. So two people died that day. Also Rivera, Donna (Agnes) and Lisa were also pregnant but they all had abortions I'm sure. So there can be added to the list three more deaths I'm not responsible for."

Heidnik's account of the deaths is a "textbook" analysis of the empty social personality. In none of his words is there any sense of his responsibility, or the slightest suggestion of remorse. At Heidnik's trial, I spent more time on the stand then anyone. The longest testimony other than mine was for two hours. I spent seven or eight hours testifying, and carefully.

I reviewed the history of mental illness based on Heidnik's hallucinations and delusional thinking, his 22 hospitalizations and 13 suicide attempts. From all that, what was reported by the news media appeared in the *Philadelphia Inquirer* on June 24, 1988. They reported only that Gary Heidnik did not speak for two and one half years because "the devil put a cookie in

his throat," I was quoted as having stated that from 1981 to 1983 Heidnik was totally "mute" for 30 months while confined at Fairview State Hospital for the Criminally Insane. In essence that is what the public learned. My testimony laid a basis for the insanity defense. I'd spent 8 months researching and developing 217 separate incidents recorded in Heidnik's history of insanity. I was absolutely sure he was insane. The jury said I was wrong. They found him guilty of murder and sentenced him to die in the electric chair. The world in general, and the universe of mental health professionals was not then, and may still not ready to accept the category of ritualistic serial killer.

After the trial, I still communicated with Heidnik several times a week. The letters he sent me are the basis for this book. Is Gary Heidnik insane or just an expert manipulator? He has told me he is repulsed by the crimes he'd committed, and the sensationalism. Heidnik said, "I'm ashamed and discussed with what happened, and have no intentions of writing a book, making any speeches, news casts, etc. All this sensational publicity has caused me to be beaten up three times and landed me on death row."

He went on to say,"...nobody believes these two deaths were not murders but accidents. They think I deliberately committed murder with a pair of handcuffs. If I'd really wanted to kill I'd have used a gun or knife or something but because of all the adverse publicity such logic is beyond people. I'm sorry but I am not available for a book, but thank you very much for your extensive help at my trial." *He signed that letter G.M. Kill not Gary M. Heidnik.*

Gary Heidnik claims that he is not a ritualistic or serial killer. He was extremely offended after reading the article that I wrote on serial killers . He stated that it,"...grieves me to be referred to by the label of serial killer. I am by no means a serial killer. Those two deaths were purely accidental. There was no willful intent or premeditation on my part to kill anyone."

In a real sense I can believe that *initially* he did not want to

kill the women. He wanted to punish them, but he did not want to kill them. He wanted to control them, and for that he needed them alive. But when the first murder occurred he discovered the ultimate control, and the inner world grew.

There is a very giving and warm side to Heidnik, the *Gary* side. But the flip side to Gary is *G.M. Kill*, a dark person with no regard for life, love of God, and a person with a dark soul. In between the two is *bishop Gary*, the intellectual, manipulative and effective person with an IQ near 150.

Heidnik is a person driven by his delusional fantasies. His various personalities were fueled by needs that had to be fulfilled. The need for closeness, and the need to be wanted was filled in the character of Bishop Gary, and his church. Those people who were his congregation loved him. He preached, he fed them and in turn they adored him. The same needs, but overshadowed by the need for control created G.M. Kill. G.M. Kill had sex slaves chained in the basement while Bishop Gary held services upstairs. *Heidnik is not, and never was, a multiple personality. His personalities are not fully distinct, rather they are characteristics of different personalities.*

These characters were developed in the fantasy and later used to disguise, hide and prevent the capture of the serial killer. He is not a fully independent multiple personality in the classic sense. He is psychotic, and more importantly a *serial killer*. The characteristics of "the Heidniks" are extreme exaggerated modes. Each mode being extreme and acting independent of one another. At the time of the trial, I was not aware of the distinctiveness of these personalities, and how they explained the enigma of Gary Heidnik.

Heidnik is also a master manipulator. He operates within his own set of norms, his own reality. Bishop Gary Heidnik can talk to God and hold church services upstairs at the same time hostages are chained naked to the pipes in his basement dungeon. He can simultaneously feed his hostages generic brand dog food in the basement, and treat his mostly retarded pa-

rishioners to a smorgasbord at a local eatery called Duffy's. Heidnik appears to be arrested on the same maturity level as that of an adolescent. He wants to appear that he is sorry and remorseful.

He appeared on TV with John Douglas of the FBI attempting to show that he is sick of what he did. "It wasn't my fault, after all all I wanted to do was to create life." In reality, he is disappointed that he never fulfilled his fantasy and his intimacy needs. He never created his own society after all. His explanation is just like the explanation you would hear from an adolescent playing catch in the backyard with a hard ball who has broken a window. The "Gary" in Gary Heidnik only wanted to create life... babies. G. M. Kill had no problem with the deaths. The victims deserved it for coming with him in the first place. Bishop Gary was the deity to be worshipped. He was in control. He had the direct line to God. The bishop was to be master of his own society.

Heidnik was tested during a G.M. Kill phase by court psychiatrist, Eva Wojecheski. She warned of his anger, paranoia, hate and disregard for authority. She saw him as a real danger. Many competent psychologists and psychiatrists warned of G.M. Kill. They did not identify the personality as "G.M. Kill ," but they saw the impending doom.

Wayne Blodgett and Al Levitt were the court psychologists from Philadelphia who evaluated Heidnik. They found him to be "delusional, paranoid, and that he had an intermittent loss of reality ... I would recommend a long term, strictly supervised inpatient psychiatric care.

Levitt and Blodgett [November 17, 1978] went on to say of Heidnik:

> ... appeared to be manipulative, he is certainly lacking in judgment. Impresses me as one who

sees himself superior to others although he must involve himself with those inferior to himself.... It is my opinion, based on extensive investigation, that he is not only a danger to himself, but perhaps a greater danger to the community, especially to those who he perceives as being weak and dependent.

CHAPTER 10

A FUNCTIONAL ANALYSIS OF THE BEHAVIOR

The mind of a serial killer is filled by his ritualistic fantasies. To enter the mind's fantasy can only be accomplished by carefully analyzing the "known behavior" of the murderer. We should submit the subject, or the evidence, to a complete functional analysis. This functional analysis is accomplished by examining antecedent behavior, the behavior itself, and the consequences of that behavior.

This can be initiated by attempting to review of the evidence from a stimulus-response point of view, i.e., by assuming that for every stimulus there is a response, another stimulus followed by another response. In the serial killer the rituals are fueled by the internal and external behaviors, and eventually lead to the murder. Each time the serial killer succeeds it increases the future probability that he will again engage in the same behavior.

Although the rituals and the reinforcement are often *only* in the internal fantasy of the serial killer, antecedent behavior gives us the only key to this otherwise private world. B.F. Skinner reminds us, in *Science and Human Behavior*, that internal behaviors are subject to the same laws as external behavior.

The difficulty with stimulus response stimulus analysis is the uncontrollability especially when the serial killer is still at large. But it must be attempted and may in fact lead to the apprehension quicker then most traditional law enforcement methods.

According to Ressler, Burgess and Douglas (1985), the internal and external behaviors are described as follows:

> For descriptive purposes, we use the terms internal and external to classify the behavior indicators. Internal behaviors include thinking patterns and experiences within or unique to the individual. The internal behaviors most consistently reported over the murderer's three developmental periods were daydreams, compulsive masturbation and isolation. External behaviors are behaviors that can be observed by others. The most reported external behaviors include chronic crying, rebelliousness, stealing, cruelty to children and assaultive actions toward adults. (pg. 30)

Traditional law enforcement methods looking for opportunity and motive, for example, and searching for common aspects among the victims does not work. Obvious links in victims seen in the external world may not be helpful and in fact, may be misleading. *The commonalty between victims is found only in the internal fantasy world of the killer.* The fuel for the individual delusion is the internal reinforcer. One of the behaviors in the fantasy needing reinforcement is sexual, but it must be remembered that this sexual behavior is not based on intimacy or closeness, but on control. When the fantasy is no longer satisfying, or it lacks enough reinforcing qualities to maintain the behavior, the behavior and the fantasy needs to be expanded into the external world. The internal reinforcement drives the person to expand his internal world into a new environment.

B.F. Skinner in *Science and Human Behavior*, proved that the successful reinforcement of a behavior increases the probability that the behavior will occur again. Each successful murder means that a serial killer will kill again. Simply put, if something good happens to you, if something happens that makes you feel good, you'll do it again. For a serial killer the thoughts and images of the fantasy produce a pleasant feeling. It may in fact be the only good feelings they have, Since these killers have substituted control for intimacy, a life-long series of behaviors culminating in the ultimate control is set off. Others may choose to explain this process in terms of cognitive mapping, they are not in opposition. This behavioral approach is offered because I believe it simplifies and, to a great extent demystifies the process.

In the November 10,1992 PBS *Frontline* interview, John Wesley Dodd, the convicted serial killer, inadvertently detailed this process:

> ...Things just gradually progressed. I said I started exposing myself when I was 13. After a while, that wasn't fun anymore, I needed some physical contact, so I started tricking kids into touching me. That wasn't any fun anymore so I started molesting kids. Things just gradually progressed, got a little bit more serious and increased in frequency. You know, if one thing wasn't exciting anymore, I had to do something else to — to get that old feeling of excitement back.

In this state, the murderer has had innumerable successful approximations. Once the murderer expands his environment to the external world, or he begins to stalk and select a victim, the rate of internal reinforcement is go great, and is occurring at such high rate, there is actually *no ability* to return to that internal world. The actual capture, torture, rape and the

associated behavior *become* the reinforcing qualities of fantasy. Therefore, serial killers may take pictures of stacked bodies in a room, cannibalize, etc. With each performance, the rate of positive reinforcement is intensified. If the particular victim has lost the reinforcing qualities the stimulus response stimulus cycle begins again. A murder is used to fuel the fantasy.

While the ritualistic serial murderer is still in the active phase law enforcement officials must determine the reinforcing qualities of the internal fantasy in order to apprehend a serial killer. They must begin by abandoning all normal assumptions about the killer. The normal assumptions are the assumptions of police officers not serial killers. Look, once more, at one of the sketches by Harrison Marty Graham. It helps to revel his internal fantasy. He was a demonic predator who saw himself-devouring women. This drawing of Harrison Graham represent the internal conflict of the serial killer between good and evil, satan and god, and the

being or "taken beasts" that evolves.

The drawing further represents the over all conflict that the serial murderer has in his mind. The internal world gives a

great deal of sexual reinforcement or pleasure to these fantasies, while the external world fights the dreams. Once the fantasy needs more fuel, the internal world's need for sexual reinforcement overpowers any attempt of external control.

Usually church or religion is the last attempt to prevent the fantasy from moving into the external world. The beast in the picture gives a graphic representation of what interworkings of Graham's' fantasies were. It also demonstrates how he views himself in his delusional process.

The crux of Heidnik's internal conflict is acceptance; he was rejected by every social group he encountered. To achieve intimacy, one must first be accepted. Therefore in Heidnik's fantasy he was always accepted; he was always in control. Heidnik verified this conflict in his own words in a letter written to me. In it he explained his need for acceptance, but accidentally revealed his overpowering need for control.

> As my marriage had deteriorated and my relationship with the handicapped disintegrated, I was again alone. What to do? What I did you already know.. A unique way of looking at what I did in my disturbed state of mind was to create my own social group or family if you wish. It was a social group in which I was the only male, the only economic provider, the patriarch so to speak, and which was available to me 24 hours a day since I couldn't achieve a sense of belonging to any of the other existing social groups in American society, I endeavored to create my own social group. One that had to provide the things I needed, love bonding, children, companionships, etc., for instance, any time I needed to talk they were there. Where could they go? They had to listen.

In his external world, Heidnik's bridge to acceptance was an attempt to make those he selected "better off" than they were. By doing something he saw as positive for them, he could justify the abusive, violent behavior towards them. But this, as we have seen, started long before the chaining of the women in his basement. In 1976 he removed Angeanette Davidson from her neglectful family. He made her better off, and she accepted him.

Ten years later he justified his actions in his basement-dungeon by showing that Josephine Rivera gained 20 pounds, gave up her cocaine addiction and was therefore better off. Inclusive to this "better off" was being kept naked and chained, and forced into a daily sexual ritual. This constituted acceptance in his fantasy. He has these women anytime he wanted them —for sex conversation and torture. He was god, they were his servants. He supplies all their needs, they supply acceptance.

Other the serial murderers have their own representation of themselves as dominant, controlling and powerful figures. They have the power over life and death. The power and control of god. In the internal world serial murderers are god. In their fantasies and in their actual enactment of the murder they are a god. It is the only power they have ever really had. Until scientists and law enforcement agencies recognize their patterns, motives and their fantasies they will remain a mystery.

Serial killers like Harrison Marty Graham, John Wesley Dodd and Gary M. Heidnik are intelligent, manipulative, delusional and driven by their fantasies. Much more research needs to be done to further clarify the definition of diagnostic category presented here.

Law enforcement must be provided with new tools to understand and apprehend these individuals more quickly. Even more must be done so that the professional mental health practitioner can identify the problem, and communicate the

result to law enforcement officials. Then such individuals can be moved to inpatient legally-supervised care. If 22 separate mental hospitalizations and 13 suicide attempts are considered malingering and not a problem, further horrible murderers will happen.

EPILOGUE

Gary Heidnik, PN-027084-L, Philadelphia, Pennsylvania, (11-20-90) revoked practical nursing license based upon Heidnik having been found guilty and convicted of 18 felony counts.

—*Pennsylvania State Board of Nursing Newsletter, Fall 1991.*

I am what a child molester looks like. There is no dirty old man. Dirty old man does not exist. I am what a child molester looks like. I am what a serial killer looks like.

— John Wesley Dodd, *Frontline,* November 10, 1992

Appendix 1

Constitution of the United Church of the Ministers of God

The consititution of Gary Heidnik's church is reproduced here, as were all his letters, with the spelling, grammar, and syntax of the original.

Article #1; The whole name of the church is to be referred t as "The United Church of the Ministers of God" or when space saving is desirable the "United Minisrty."

Article #2; Once the church is organised and a board of directors (five) is selected, an election is to be held to determine who will be named Bishop.

Article #3; The office of Bishop is to be held for life or until the so selected chooses to resign. The Bishop will then choose those he desires to be his Councilor and his Treasurer.

Article #4; No officers of the Church are to receive pay or other compensation for services rendered. Their work is entirely voluntary.

Article #5; Bishop is to have full control and responsibility for Church funds.

Article #6; The duties of the Bishop are many and his control extensive. He is to be responsible for all activities, expansion, projects, etc. His is the final word on interpretation of The Bible or the settling of religious disputes, except for divine intervention. He will usually be able to act without the consent or notification of the board. He may hold services, select new ministers, or buildings, plan new activities or directions. He may only be thwarted by a full unanimous decision of the Board or if he violates this Constitution. If he is a member of the Board his vote in such a decision doesn't count.

Article #7; Any vacancies on the Board arising from death, illness, resignation, etc are to be filled by an election of the remaining Board members. A simple majority wins the election.

Article #8; Members of the Board are to be awarded the titles of Reverand as a means of thanking them for their services.

Article #9; During services, prayer meetings, weddings, funerals, baptismals, etc to aviod embarresment to our poorer members and avoid creating the illusion of a very mercenary organization <u>there are to be no collection dishes or donations collected, or any charges or fees for services rendered.</u>

Article #10; Money to support the Church can be raised from outside sources such as loans, stocks, bingo games, business ventures, or other endeavors.

 a. Contributions will be accepted, but only in private or in some other informal fashion such as the mails.

 b. Assets are to be used for furthering the goals of the Church such as purchase of buildings for worship, administration, education, and heat, etc.

 c. Contributions that can be asked for are those not in a materialistic sense, such as labor or advice.

Article #11; Title of Reverand is to be given somewhat freely to those who show a devout interest in spreading God's word. There are to be no requirements of formal education or restrictions based on sex, race, or age. The title can be awarded separately by the Bishop or by a majorty of the Board members.

Article #12; The Bible, both Old and New Testaments, is to be the guiding inspiration. "The New World Translation of the Holy Scriptures is to be the favored translation, but it is to be rremembered that it is only an interpretation of the original Scriptures.

Article 12; The divinity of Christ is questionable, but he is recognized as God's prophet and our Savior, hence his claim of Divine Origin is to be played down.

Article 15; When the Church obtains enough funds to obtain and maintain a fair sized house of worship, it is to be purchased or built somewhere in Philadelphia, the city our Church was first formaly organised. Any additional buildings for worship are to be purchased or built in areas where they are needed most.

Article 16; Our sacred aim is to promote the worship and teachings of God and we will endeavor to do this with two systems.

a. The more conventional technique of a church building with pews, organs, ministers, etc.

b. The much more ancient idea of small groups of individuals coming together in the home or elsewhere and praying. To give these meetings a small air of officiality the leaders of these meetings are to be given the title of Deacon or Reverand.

Article #17; Any new laws, amendments, or changes made to this Constitutionmust be approved by a two-thirds majority of the Board, but may be vetoed irrevocably by the Bishop.

Article #18; If and when dissolution of should ever become necessary, the total assets of the Church should be given directly or sold and the profits given equaly to the Federal Government's Peace Corps and Veterens Administration.

Appendix 2

Intimacy and Control

Adapted from *The Intimacy Manual,* Edmund T. Amidon, et.al., International Information Associates, Inc. 1992.

Wherever we are now in our lives, we can think of where we have been, where we are and where we are going as scenes in a journey from birth to death. Along the way we take part in relationships with others. We see...we meet...we talk...we experience...we compete...we fall in love...we separate. We move through many relationships. In all of it we are singular individuals with our own perceptions of ourselves and our performance, our perceptions of others and their performance, and even our own perceptions or guesses of their perceptions.

When we begin to relate to another person we wonder what the future will be. Will the relationship be related to control or to intimacy? Will I attempt to control, to share control or to give up control to this other person? Wanting intimacy or control in a relationship is not a static condition. In every relationship we move back and forth between intimacy and control in varying degrees. If a relationship is to grow and develop, not only is our choice of intimacy or control important, but also how we express our desires for intimacy and/or control.

We tend to pair intimacy and control. Could that be right... are they not at opposite poles? They seem far apart, and yet the conditions for striving for either one of them are so close as to be identical. What is the common thread that keeps intimacy and control so closely entwined? The desire for intimacy and the desire for control both test and stretch us intellectually, emotionally and physically. Passion is the connection, our zest for living, the life motivator, the catalyst. We humans will have these times of passion again and again in our lives. Our goal in this book is to create a structure for understanding our relationships with others. The ideas used to create the structure are intimacy and control.

In relating to others we have the potential to learn more and more about ourselves. We gain information about how we are perceived by others and how we behave toward others. We receive feedback on our actions toward or against others; we get involved and relieve our loneliness. We attract people and repel them, and in turn are attracted and repelled, but we shall relate and be passionate.

We are all creatures with personal frameworks, rituals, and systems. When we can arrange information to fit into our own personal understanding or framework we create comfort and feelings of control within ourselves. We are about to introduce frameworks that you may want to add to your personal maps and charts.

These frameworks interrelate as a three dimensional system for looking at our relationship behavior, taking into account the intellectual, the emotional and the physical/behavioral aspects of each of us.

Control is one of the two major concepts that will be used to consider our behavior. This concept is often thought about in terms of being at a "higher level." A person who feels (s)he has less control or power than another might complain that the other "looks down on me."

We have all heard of people who, when they feel intimidated or fall in love, tend to place the other person upon a pedestal. At the same time, when people are feeling superior or in greater control they may place themselves upon the pedestal looking down upon the other person. At still other times, the two individuals stand face to face and relate on equal terms. This may be thought of as a pedestal theory of communication. We tend to relate to each other based on our concept of ourselves in relation to another and our perceptions of the way that other relates to us.

If this scheme sounds familiar, it's because it is based on and similar to Eric Berne's Transactional Analysis concepts of parent, adult and child. When I am feeling ONE-UP, I am feeling better (more powerful) than you, and in my eyes you are ONE-DOWN. My communication and behavior in relation to you will be affected by this inner judgment. If I am feeling ONE-DOWN, I am placing myself below you and will behave toward you as though I am less than you. If I am feeling that we are EVEN with each other I can relate to you directly and without manipulation. This seems simple, but keep in mind that one's own *perception* of the relationship at a given time is just that: an individual's perception. The object of my attention also has his/her perceptions with regard to him/herself and me. In relationships it is important to be aware of our own perceptions and also conscious of the perceptions of others. We may consider our relationships as being in one of three arenas: family, friendship, or organizational.

FOUNDATIONS OF INTIMACY AND CONTROL BEHAVIORS

When we enter into a relationship, intimacy and control are among the most important issues we will need to consider: how close to be, and how to exercise control in the relationship.

These two great human issues seem always with us in our

contacts with others. In our more involved and lasting relations, whether focused on friendship, work or love, these two key elements appear to dominate our concerns.

Several questions should be used to focus our attention on these issues:

- What do we want and expect from a close relationship?
- What are our attitudes toward control and intimacy?
- How are these attitudes related to one another?
- What barriers exist that affect these relationships?

Consideration of these questions helps us understand our face to face relationships.

We have chosen to look at our goals, attitudes, perceptions and behaviors to describe our relationships in terms of intimacy and control. Finally, how can we describe our goals, attitudes and assumptions about intimacy and control? These questions form the focus the study.

Our ideas and experiences of intimacy and control in social interaction do suggest answers to these questions. Information (data) we have collected provides a basis for speculating about these relationships.

GOALS, EXPECTATIONS, ATTITUDES, ASSUMPTIONS AND SYMBOLS

At some level the use of these words is confused and confusing. Perhaps this is reasonable considering the overlapping meaning of many words and ideas that we use to characterize our relationships. Consider the following statement made by a man who is about to marry:

"I want to settle down and have a real friend (my wife to be), someone I can share my feelings, thoughts and experi-

ences with. I expect to have and want to have a really close relationship. That's what a marriage is two people who can share, trust, enjoy and grow in appreciation of one another."

This statement provides an example of each of those words that are basic to the understanding of the concepts.

This person has a *goal* in mind for the relationship, stated in terms of what he wants. The statement itself offers some detail about the type of relationship he wants with the person he is planning to marry.

In this case the *expectation* is apparently closely linked to the *goal.* The person expects to achieve the goal. That is, it is his *expectation* that the type of relationship he wants will exist when the marriage occurs. He is clearly making certain *assumptions* about the intended partner, and perhaps about marriage itself. The assumptions are closely related to his expectations; he assumes certain qualities are characteristic of his future wife and marriage, and therefore expects that certain things will happen in the marriage.

The person's attitudes toward relationships and specifically intimacy are also clear. An *attitude* may be thought of as a predisposition to act, or a way of thinking and feeling about something, similar to a belief. The person's attitude toward intimacy can be described as positive, at least in the context of marriage.

The *symbol* is important because it is often thought of as what we want, but may merely stand for what we are really trying to achieve. In the situation presented, marriage could represent the desired relationship, and in that sense marriage is the symbol.

In general, people seem to want and expect two things from a relationship: to be treated fairly, and to be close. In other words, our relationship goals, or what we personally want from relationships, lie mainly in the areas of intimacy

and control. Often we understand these goals more in terms of symbols than in the reality of intimacy or control. To many, marriage is more a symbol of intimacy than the real thing.

People do seek intimacy and control in their relationships with others. Often the search is not for power over a person or closeness to a person, but rather for achievement of the symbols of power or intimacy. The goals that people expect to attain in relationships seem as many and varied as the number of relationships in the world.

What do we expect and want from a relationship? Some common goals are stated in terms of intimacy. Think about some of the statements people make about what they want in life:

"I want to be married"

"I want to share my life with another person"

"I want a good family"

"I want to have *support* from someone in a close relationship"

"I want a good sexual relationship"

"I want companionship —I fear loneliness"

"I want an attractive lover"

"I want a physical relationship —lots of touching"

"I want to be accepted as I am"

"I want someone to tell my troubles to"

These are some common goals people try to achieve in relationships, as well as many of the satisfactions people expect in their closest relationships.

What kinds of power and control do we want and expect in our relationships? People do need, want and expect power

and control over their lives, and see close relationships as having something to do with getting what they want. Consider the following types of statements:

"I want to feel confident"

"I would like not to have to worry about money"

"I want to get a good education"

"I want to have the necessary things for the good life"

"I don't want demands placed on me"

"I want to feel important"

"I want to have a good job"

"I want to feel that when I compete I win"

"I want to be strong"

"I want to be treated fairly and to be equal"

The point of presenting such specific issues is to show that most of us do want and expect rather specific outcomes from relationships. Also, we can see from these lists that what we want and expect is easily thought of in two general categories, Intimacy and Control.

ARE OUR SYMBOLS REAL?

Closely related to our goals for intimacy and control are the *symbols* that represent the actual goals. No one really feels that symbols alone produce happiness, but often the symbol is pursued as though it were the actual goal.

Sometimes the goal and symbol can be combined. Perhaps the best example is marriage. Marriage may be thought of as a symbol of intimacy. Often people will ask others, "Are you married?" Another way of asking this question might be,

"Are you involved in an intimate relationship that would put limits on any close relationship I might have with you?"

Symbols for power are well known. Perhaps the most important is money. Of course money is not only a symbol but in most circumstances it is also the instrument of power. This may be most clearly expressed by the phrase "everyone has his price," which implies that if you have enough money you can control anyone.

Often it is the symbol that we seek, and confuse the symbol with the goal. When we get it we realize that the symbol was not what we wanted, but only represented something we wanted or thought we wanted.

We define a symbol of intimacy or control as something (an object, idea, person, relationship) that represents the goal. The goal is to meet our needs for closeness to another, or needs to control the self and/or the life environment. So a symbol is not what the person really wants, but is seen as having some very basic connection with the real goal.

Some common symbols of intimacy are marriage, a ring, a bed, a kiss, an embrace and a gift. Symbols of power include money, awards, big cars, gavels, firm handshakes, loud voices, and a clenched fist. Some symbols of intimacy may also be seen as symbols of control. The reverse does not appear to be true.

Responsive Control

Most people desire closeness and equality, under certain conditions. The attitudes we hold toward the interaction of intimacy and control could be expressed as, "If I let myself be known to others, I will lose some of my power with them. When people know me I will be vulnerable and thus weakened." Of course, the theme of this expression is, "I'm not sure of myself." Getting to know someone involves revealing and finding out about weaknesses and other aspects of the self

thought not to be good. Many of our strongest resistances toward intimacy have to do with being careful, cautious, and suspicious. It is fairly clear that as a person becomes concerned with having control, he or she will also increase defenses against closeness.

ANALYSIS OF MESSAGES

"I want to get to know you better."

"I am concerned about where this relationship is going."

"I'm involved with my own goals."

"We may be too involved with each other."

These phrases are all from the normal everyday world of talking, but also represent a special type of talking most frequently heard in close relationships.

We assume that:

- Attention to what we say and how we say it will help us understand the consequences of our statements.
- Seeing words as tools in communication will help us to use words with sensitivity to their impact on others.
- Understanding our overall pattern of communication will lead us to greater satisfaction and success in our close relations.
- Listening to our own statements from the other person's perspective will give us greater control over ourselves.
- Reading the message of another person carefully, using all the cues the other sends along with talking, will help us understand what others are thinking, feeling and saying. And finally, by becoming a careful moni-

tor of our own conversations with others, we will significantly improve our opportunities for getting what we want out of our relationships. Understanding our relationships is a key to self knowledge.

THE INTIMACY AND CONTROL CONNECTION

Intimacy and control may be used to describe our behavior. This behavior that we engage in is for many people the *goal of life;* that is, *to feel close and powerful* in important relationships. An important way of looking at our behavior is analysis of our talking.

We assume that the processes of our own interaction are related to our attitudes, goals, perceptions and expectations. By looking at control and intimacy in the actual communication processes, we can gain an understanding of how behavior is related to the direction of conversation and become more skillful in reaching our own goals.

There seem to be general patterns of control and intimacy behavior that we *all* expect, depending on the situation. For example, most of us expect that at a party we might "break the ice" with small talk, but that if we are attracted to someone and become more personal in our talk the reactions from the other person might also become more intimate, and that a pattern toward continued intimacy might develop.

We also might expect that in a work situation with a subordinate, our pattern might at first include providing information, orientation, suggestion and then eventually become directive and corrective. Much depends on our own individual goals and attitudes, *but once conversation or interaction has begun, the interaction itself becomes an important cause of what follows.* That's why it's so important to be aware of the patterns as they develop.

The development of the intimacy pattern generally moves

in the direction of a feeling of closeness over time. In a simple almost self evident sense the more time spent in talking about interpersonal topics, the more likely it is that the talk will either stop or become more intimate. The pattern of intimacy will move from topics of interest significant to the speaker to talk about the speakers' individual lives to talk about one another.

People may talk about their interests, such as sports and music, at some length. Probably individual experience will become part of the conversation at some point. For many relationships, this part of a pattern will be the focus of conversation. In a sense people share their experience with one another. This is an important part of intimacy in most relationships, that is, talking to someone about experiences you have had that the listener has not experienced.

For example, when two young people (a boy and a girl) first meet, they may talk at length about school, music they like, and places to go. They also may begin to say things about how their parents treat them, their friends, and their own personal tastes. (Certainly after a date or two they will.) By the time they are "steadies," most of their talk will be about themselves and each other — a lot of it about good and bad feelings they have and wonder about in the other.

Adults who meet at a social gathering will likely talk at first about very general topics and continue to do so with enjoyment even after frequent meetings. Two men will talk about sports, politics, business, maybe religion, women in general, etc. After they have become good friends, they will occasionally speak about the private thoughts and feelings they have about their wives, children, themselves and each other.

If a male "smooth operator" meets an attractive woman at a club, he will probably start talking in an outwardly very intimate manner. It may seem insincere or too forward to the woman, so she may leave or ask him to leave, in words or by her cool manner (the brush off). If not, and if they are at-

tracted to each other, the conversation may begin with the expression of compliments, feelings and desires, but it will probably become less intimate after a while as they back off for a time to get to know each other better. They will talk about their personal lives and experiences, and feelings about others in their lives. After a while, they may move to quite deep levels of personal intimacy, speaking verbally and non-verbally only about each other and feelings.

In all of these situations it appears as though the desire for intimacy is the motivation for the interaction. Perhaps some situations appear to be focused primarily on intimacy and others on control, but of course the apparent focus of nearly all conversation is some mixture. Just as the examples presented here seemed to be concerned with intimacy, we are all aware of situations where the concern appears to be control: Think of the salesman who talks in a ringing, steady "charming" stream of words. Think of the friend who uses big words and abstract ideas, leaving you to admire him in a way, but also to feel excluded and a little disgusted. Recall the person in a meeting who never stops to take a breath so that no one else can get in a word without creating a scene or the ingenuous person who talks about highly interesting or important topics, never stopping. Listeners feel internal pressure not to interrupt. *All these persons are in fact controlling their listeners with their talk,* though one might recognize that the listeners are in a sense agreeing to comply, or the situation couldn't take place.

THE CONNECTION BETWEEN INTIMACY AND CONTROL

There appears to be a relationship between intimacy and control, and it's difficult to tell when we want one of the two to the exclusion of the other. So if a person is talking about personal experience, and if the listener is involved at times exchanges his/her own experience, then the focus of control remains flexible.

A clear indicator of verbal control is the amount of talk. If the roles are talker-listener, then talking simply becomes the instrument of control. Telling about one's experience, ideas, or beliefs becomes the controlling agent in conversations.

Generally, the amount of talk becomes controlling particularly when it appears that one person is the talker and the other the listener, and the roles of the participants do not change. Perhaps control becomes an issue in relationships and groups when the balance of participation is such that one person is talking nearly all the time and the other person is not participating verbally. When one of the participants in a conversation does most of the talking, then he/she may also determine the *level* at which the conversation exists. Intimacy and control levels are likely to remain at what might be termed typical, normal, or average in most conversations. By simply exchanging information about experiences that the participants in the conversation have had with others but not with one another, this "average" level of intimacy is maintained.

Under these conditions, control is exerted through talking and the intimacy level is maintained by sharing something that *one* member but not necessarily both feels is significant.

These conditions exist for much of the conversation that we are part of in our daily lives. That is, conversations are not made up of statements that seem to specifically suggest either control or intimacy. The person talking about experiences is referring to those that happened in the past or with people not present. The intimacy message is not stated directly, but rather is suggested indirectly. The same seems true of control. The control message is not sent directly, but rather by focusing the conversation the talker maintains control over the agenda and thus the listener.

THE LEVELS OF VERBAL INTIMACY TECHNIQUE (LOVIT)

Most intentional human communication seems to be verbal. How can we develop an understanding of what happens when people talk (communicate verbally)? Systematic observation of talking in small groups can help us understand what people are doing and how as members and leaders we can gain more insight into our own relationships with others. Systematic awareness of our own behavior is fundamentally valuable in making decisions about how we will behave.

The focus of this section is on the development of intimacy behavior in a group. One way to approach the problem is to classify the things people say and do with each other along a continuum from least intimate to most intimate.

Ten categories or *levels of behavior* in a group are scaled from least intimate to most intimate. The intimacy continuum extends from level one (least intimate) to level ten (most intimate).

Level 1: Silence, no single conversation

This first level is used to describe a group when members are carrying on more than one conversation simultaneously. The situation is affected somewhat by group size. In smaller groups of two to five persons we are somewhat less likely to find several conversations at the same time. Included in level one is the situation when *no* member of the group is talking.

This level of verbal intimacy is used when there is *no single* discussion going on within the group. The group does not look or sound like a group. Members sit in *silence*, or in smaller groups. People may be sitting passively with little movement, often looking away from others.

Another type of behavior at this level is *noise*. Noise occurs when two or more members are talking at the same time. This

includes periods when people interrupt each other, or when one member starts to talk while another member is still talking and the interrupted member continues to talk.

Two or more simultaneous conversations presents another example of Category One. This may be observed in what appears to be a single group formation, one person is interacting with a part of the group. If there are only two people in the group, this category is applied somewhat differently. In the case of a couple or other two person group, both members may be in the same place at the same time, but they are not talking to one another. Examples of this occur throughout the lives of most married couples; one of the members of a couple may be talking while the other is reading or watching TV. A common experience in a marriage relationship is for the two partners to be together in the same place and yet for both to have their thoughts focused somewhere other than the relationship or the other person.

Level 2: Small Talk, verbal exchange

Level 2 includes many of the kinds of things that people talk about when they don't know each other very well. Basically, this level includes those things that people talk about when they are *not talking about their own present or past experience.*

In some ways this category contains statements that do not clearly fit into any of the other categories. Statements concerned with people and their relationships in general, statements about the group and about those experiences members have had outside the group are *not included* at this level. Even with the above restrictions, there are many examples of statements in this category in all of our daily conversations.

Those statements that we often think of as small talk, or cocktail-party talk are included in this lowest level of verbal intimacy. Level 2 statements are about topics that concern us but over which we have little or no control, and no involvement except perhaps as observers. We are all aware of the weather

and it effects, but we don't participate in it except as observers, victims or beneficiaries.

A conversation at this level of intimacy could include any one of a large number of topics or issues that people talk about when they are at meetings, informal gatherings or in work relationships. Some examples of these topics are the academic disciplines, sciences, language, art, music, automobiles, houses, yards, nature, sports, and important people. Specific discussions about individuals not known by members of the group, like political figures or famous people, fall in this category. Discussion about much of what appears in the newspapers would be included in Level 2. Expressions of feelings, values and attitudes are included in this category if the value, feeling or attitude is expressed toward someone or something that is not part of a member's experience. Examples would be feelings about or attitudes toward the President, war, the United Nations, or movies. Also included are statements of feelings or attitudes toward things in a person's life such as food or the weather.

Level 3: People in General

This category includes discussions about people and their relationships. Such topics as leadership, membership, conflict in groups and issues of interpersonal relations also are located in this category. Included are discussions about the nature and function of different kinds of groups such as committees, therapy, encounter, sensitivity, men's, women's, professional, business, educational and family groups. The main guideline to follow in using this category is that *statements refer to groups or relationships among people in general and do not refer to specific people or relationships among specific people.* If a statement refers to ideas about groups or interpersonal relations in general, it probably belongs in this category. If it refers to a *specific group or interpersonal situation that the speaker has experienced,* then it belongs in another category.

Level 4: Outside the group: Individual experience

The talking classified in Level 4 is *personal to the speaker*. It is psychologically close to the speaker, but may not be close to the listener. It does have an effect on the listener(s) that may help the listener feel close to the speaker.

"If the speaker sounds like the kind of person I can trust, then I will probably want to say something about myself."

Level 4 statements are more intimate than Level 3 statements because of personal involvement of one member with the topic of conversation. *The more people are involved in the content of a discussion, the more involved they will become with the members of a group.*

The first thing many people think about telling others is something about their life and experience outside the present group. Any time a person is talking about personal experiences rather than expressing feelings about his or her life, this category is used. The category includes personal background information and facts about what has happened to a person.

Level 5: Outside the Group: Shared Experience

Level 5 is more intimate than Level 4 because *those things being talked about are personal experiences for more than just one member of the group.* The personal experience "shared by part of the group" may also be of interest to other group members because of the fact that when a subgroup from a larger group meets, its topic of conversation often becomes "the rest of the group." Level 5 includes all statements regarding subgroups of the membership that have gotten together outside the group. It also includes statements about future activities group members will share outside of the group. Statements of this nature do not require the outside activity to be group related. This category may provide information about subgroups that exist outside of the group. Information of this nature may be helpful in determining the structure of subgroups operating

within the group as well. Level 5 is considered mid-range on the intimacy scale because it represents statements that have some group centered content. However, this content may be minimal, given that discussion probably does not refer to the group as a whole, is not in reference to the present situation, and is not necessarily directly associated with feelings.

Level 6: Group Experience: Past, Future, Hypothetical

The focus of this category is the present group. The statements included are: (a) about the past, (b) the future, and (c) general statements about the present group.

One of the most important topics groups discuss is their immediate past experience. *For this category system the past is defined as anything that occurred before the beginning of the present meeting.* Therefore, when people are discussing things that happened at a previous group meeting held earlier in the same day or the day before, such talk would be classified in this category.

Level 7: Outside the group: Feelings About Individual Experience

This category includes expressions of a group member's feelings about events in her/his life outside of the group. Usually, statements of this nature will be made in the first person. Another member of the group may seek to clarify material in this category. Attempts may also be made to probe more deeply into the incident and its effects. Such actions by other members often are in the form of questions, open ended statements, or empathic remarks. *Any verbal interaction that serves to keep the group focus on the incident* is classified in Level 7. Only statements *expressing emotion about incidents not related to the group* are included in Level 7.

Level 8: Inside the group: Indirect Expression of Feeling

Level 8 talk includes expression of feeling that is indirectly stated, does not clearly say that the feeling is the speaker's, and

does not include clear labeling or naming of the feeling. Feeling is said to be expressed indirectly when the criteria of ownership of feeling and labeling the feeling are not met. The most frequently used ways to express feelings indirectly are through the expression of value, opinion, question, reference and tone of voice. *Levels and statements that place values* on the group, people in the group, or things that have been said in the group. These are most often made with reference to whether a thing is good or bad, or appropriate or inappropriate. Another way to think about these statements is that they are related to standards that members of the group have or have not met. These statements usually include words like good, right, appropriate, wrong, bad, mistake, and sometimes "I can't agree with you."

A second type of statement that falls into this category involves explaining one's behavior or apologizing. When members explain to the group or a person in the group why they did something, the statement is placed in Level 8. Another behavior that indicates indirect expression of feeling is a statement that communicates denial of feeling. This category does not imply the existence of a feeling in all cases, but the act of denial does indicate that the speaker probably has some feeling (discomfort, resistance) about being labeled as having the feelings. Classification in this category is much clearer when the verbal behavior is supported by some nonverbal indicator. Therefore, the statement needs to be made in such a way that the tone of voice or some other quality of the voice makes it clear that the person is expressing a feeling. Another method of expressing feelings and emotions indirectly is through a *reference* to another or others. The feeling is indirect because the criterion of *ownership of the feeling* is not met the person allows others to represent his/her feelings. When a person expresses feelings in this way it is not clear that the feeling really belongs to the speaker. The speaker makes ownership of the feeling unclear through the use of an indefinite or uncertain reference to the owner of the feeling.

Level 9: Inside the Group: Description of Experience

All statements describing the "here and now" experience of the group are placed in this category. These types of verbal interaction can be broken down into more specific behaviors. Here and now experiences are defined as events happening at the moment as well as anything which occurred during the present meeting. Descriptive statements are used when people want to talk about their shared experiences. It also includes the following types of statements:

a) Statements that attempt to clarify or restate a statement made by another person, for example, "I hear you saying that the group is working on its problem."

b) Statements that are group oriented and deal with events and activities which are occurring or have occurred in the present meeting. Conversation of this type is often used to analyze feelings or attitudes that are present in a relationship.

Level 10: Inside the Group: Direct Expression of Feeling

The ideas that seem most central to intimacy may be best illustrated by behavior in this category. Earlier, we suggested that the most intimate types of conversation are focused inside a group or relationship. When people are speaking *to* those they are talking about, and when they are expressing their feelings directly, then their conversation is at the highest level of intimacy.

This category at the extreme of the continuum includes those statements that are *most intimate*. The criteria that must be met therefore include the here and now criteria met for the previous category, but also include others. Specifically the criteria for Level 10 are (1) Direct statement to the person or group, (2) *Here and now* expression of feeling, (3) Clear ownership of the feeling by speaker, and (4) The use of a *feeling related word*.

The categories for Levels of Verbal Intimacy Technique

(LOVIT) have been designed for use in training and self understanding. This method can be used to help gain insight into the levels of intimacy that groups achieve, and processes that both facilitate and inhibit intimate verbal interaction. Specifically, the instrument can be used as:

1. A *guide* for group leaders to use in facilitating a group. A group leader who knows the LOVIT method will be able to talk in ways that produce levels of intimacy which are helpful to the group.

2. A *tool* for assessing group problems. A leader or the members of groups can examine the group's own conversation and identify particular patterns of development that seem to produce problems.

3. A *method for focusing interaction* in groups that have intimacy as a goal (such as marriage or friendship). Many kinds of groups are concerned with intimacy. Perhaps the group that talks most about intimacy is the marriage counseling group. In this group the members are usually trying to reach a level of intimacy that is satisfying to both partners. The LOVIT can be used to discover the levels that each partner uses, thus focusing on differences that exist between partners. It can help both partners determine methods for developing mutually satisfying levels of intimacy.

4. A *goal-setting device* for use in groups. If a group (a couple, training group, support group, etc.) identifies improvement of communication as a goal, members can use LOVIT to select specific intimacy patterns they wish to practice and achieve.

LEVELS OF VERBAL CONTROL TECHNIQUE

Level 1 - Silence

This level is a non-talking category. It describes an uncer-

tain condition of directiveness. It occurs when no one is talking or when several people are talking at once.

It is important to notice how long silence lasts in conversation. When do people fall silent? Silence has many meanings in a conversation. What is your reaction to silence? Some silent periods are very uncomfortable. Usually if you think carefully and objectively about what was said just before a silence, or what unusual patterns of conversation occurred before the silence, the meaning of the silence can become clear or at least some clues to its meaning will be uncovered.

In these periods of silence, people are usually thinking. In some sense this category allows for further analysis of the exchange of messages. When people are together and not talking, they are often thinking about what to say or what has been said. At times people are waiting for someone else to talk, or something to happen.

This level of behavior is used to make the continuum complete. That is, it makes the scheme useable at any time and in any situation where people are together. Silence is not a totally ambiguous class of behavior in terms of interpretation. During periods of silence people think, communicate nonverbally and generally send out and receive messages that may be seen as a part of the total communication pattern. When you use a method for analysis of directiveness in control behavior, the silence category may help in understanding overall patterns of control, resistance, conflict and resolution. A more complete analysis of the meaning of silence in communication patterns is presented later in this section. Nonverbal behavior is treated extensively in a later chapter.

Level 2 - Negative Reaction

Statements in this category include negative evaluation, criticism, reprimand, negative feelings, defensive behavior, and self-justification. Criticism, reprimand, negative evaluation and expression of negative feelings are all considered *directive ex-*

pression of control. In what sense are these statements directive? Why are critical, negative, evaluative and reprimand statements so significant in a concept of power, control and authority? When we think of control or power, we think of directive-oriented organizations. Historically, military, religious, corporate and governmental organizations operate on the principle of direction from the top down. The words used are most extreme when the direction or directiveness must be focused on errors, mistakes, or corrections. Statements of negative reaction or evaluation send the message that "your behavior is wrong, mistaken, erroneous or just unacceptable, and don't do it any more."

In a sense, negative evaluation or reaction is focused and directive in that it communicates what one must *not* do, and that doing certain things is not correct or appropriate. Criticism is directive in that it indicates that there are limits, and that one must change behavior to fit the standards.

The reaction to criticism is frequently negative. It is often said that it's all right to criticize, but few like to be the recipients of criticism.

Often negative evaluation is expressed in such a way that it elicits a defensive reaction. When criticized, a person often feels defensive and at the same time feels that he/she *should not* feel defensive because the evaluating person is really "trying to help."

We associate evaluation with authority. Leaders of all kinds have as part of their roles the evaluation of their subordinates. When the subordinates do not meet standards, make mistakes, or perform inappropriately the authority or person in control criticizes or reprimands. It is particularly easy to see, therefore, that parents, teachers, managers, administrators, and officers of various types are critical and often directive. Negative evaluation is something that can include a large element of non-talking behavior as well. The *tone of voice* can be the primary carrier of the question: "What are you doing?"

This statement appears to be a request for information, but if it is said with a particular tone of voice the message is really: "What you are doing is wrong."

The eyes and the voice are both carriers of messages. Many people use the "stare" to communicate disapproval. The face is a powerful communicator of the message. A smile or lack of it can greatly change the meaning of the message, particularly if the words are strongly negative. Consider this example:

"You are making a big mistake. I think that you are wrong, and totally inappropriate. It's going to get you into a whole lot of trouble."

This message is sent with a smile. What does the receiver think and feel when the message is sent with a smile? First of all, the message is extremely direct. The person receiving can have little doubt about the desires of the person doing the reprimanding. There seems to be clarity about what the speaker *does not want* the receiver to do. But what about the smile? Its inclusion opens the message to interpretation. Does the smile mean that the critical message is not so critical, or does it mean the sender wants to include a positive message with the negative?

Perhaps the greatest problem in this type of message is the possibility that the smile will confuse the receiver. For example, "perhaps the smile means that he is enjoying criticizing me." Of course there can be an unlimited number of meanings associated with any message. The more discrepant the words and the physical behavior, the more likely people are to receive a wide range of messages. A more extensive discussion of this topic is included in the section on nonverbal behavior.

Level 3 - Corrective Feedback

Statements in this category give information. They tell you what you are doing that's wrong, why it's in error, and how to

do it right or correct it. Level 3 is considered to be the next most directive category. It includes statements that send the following message(s):

a) Something is missing and/or some error has been made.

b) You need certain information to change or do it better.

c) This is the information you need.

d) This is why you need the information.

The statement does provide corrective information for the receiver in the sense that emphasis is placed on information rather than the error. The feedback given in correction allows the receiver to operate without greater or increased direction or criticism. Corrective feedback differs from the negative reaction in that the feedback is specific and focused on the reason for the correction. These statements may also differ from negative evaluation because of the lack of disapproval in the statement. This does not mean that corrective feedback is not often perceived as negative, rather that the emphasis in this category is on information: What is the error, and why it needs to be corrected.

Level 4 - Direction, Instruction, Command

A direction is of course directive but does not in and of itself mean or communicate anything about something wrong, an error, or a mistake. The direction leaves no doubt about what the speaker wants. The message of the direction is specific. Sometimes the direction includes specific details (when, where and how). Directions are often short and to the point.

Level 5 - Suggestion, Advice, or Wishes

Statements in this category often use words like you *could*, *should* or *ought to* do this or that. These statements are similar to directions but differ in that they are less specific. Often advice is given as a "wish" after something has happened:

"I wish you had told me about that."

The message that an advice or suggestion statement usually carries is you should try to do it another way. The *ought* or *should* is usually included in the statement or it is understood:

- Buy from the supermarket. Don't go to the gourmet shop any more, it's too expensive.

The "you should" is clearly a part of the message. Some people have suggested that advice and suggestions are really just indirect criticisms or directions:

- Why don't you try taking the bus?
- You know I think you should have told him that.
- It ought to be easy for you to go back and ask for your money back.
- I think you could get a lot out of a course on 'how to get along with people'.

Level 6 - Information, facts, opinions, ideas and thoughts about many things

This is a broad category, and includes much of what we talk about. It includes facts, ideas and opinions about almost everything. The general category that we call *knowledge* or *facts* is included here.

Another type of talk in this category is about life experiences or facts about one's life. Descriptions of how the person views things, or feels, is also included here. Essentially, Level 6 emphasizes providing information. The information may either be about the speaker or it may be about some topic that is beyond the scope of the relationship or the situation. One question to use as a guide while using this category is:

Is the person just providing information to the other(s) present, or is the information embedded in a suggestion, evaluation, direction, correction or question? If the statement gives information and not a suggestion, then it is information and only information. When information is embedded in a suggestion, question, evaluation, direction, or correction, it is probably functioning as another category.

Level 7 - Question for Information

The question is nearly as common as statements which give information. In some sense they go together.

- Do you know anything about the new computers?
- What did you do after I left?
- What about the various energy sources? What sources are available?

We know that a question is a question unless it fits one of the other categories as well. The question form may actually be used in any of the other categories, so that any question is not necessarily a Level 7 question.

In order for the statement to be considered a *real* question its message should be:

"I want to get some information about ____."

Level 8 - Clarifying Question

A clarifying question is a specific type of question. It follows another person's statement. This is the kind of question that may follow a complicated point that someone has made. It is always made in response to a specific message that has been sent. The clarifying question is also fairly brief. The central message of this type of question is, "Can you clarify what you said?"

Level 9 - Acknowledging the Contributions of Others

This category includes statements that summarize, restate, or simply refer to the contribution.

The central message in this kind of accepting or acknowledging statement is, "I am *listening,* understanding, and accepting your message. I am not evaluating it. It's OK with me the way it is."

Category 9 statements focus on and are responsive to the contribution. There are many sorts of statements that fall in this category. Generally they are short, not emotionally loaded, and introduce no new content to what the speaker has said.

Level 10 - Positive Reaction

The statements in this category are not directive to the speaker, but rather are responsive to him/her. The message is, "I like what you are saying. I like you, and your ideas are good."

In some sense Level 10 statements are the opposite of those in Level 2. Included are positive evaluation, praise, support and positive feeling. The statements are not directive because they are focused on what the speaker is saying, and in fact *encourage the speaker to direct her/himself.*

This type of statement may be heard as "I am supporting you to go on and develop your ideas the way you are doing."

NONVERBAL MESSAGES OF INTIMACY AND CONTROL

Imagine eleven people seated in a circle. One of them, an immaculately groomed young man, sits stiffly, legs together, arms crossed, and says:

"I want to be close to this group. I feel very comfortable with everyone here."

The words carry a message, and his tone of voice seems to convey the same meaning, yet the rest of the group members

feel uneasy about his commitment. They feel a contradiction in his message that puts them on guard. The words sound true but the visual message his body is sending bears a different meaning. Our bodies send a constant stream of messages as we converse verbally with one another. These messages are more spontaneous and, under less conscious control than our verbal messages. The meanings of these nonverbal messages may seem subtle and imprecise, but their impact on our intended receivers may be stronger than the impact of our words. *Our nonverbal behaviors can serve to reinforce or contradict our verbal messages.* At times when our verbal messages are unclear, the nonverbal information we send may serve to bring the real message into focus.

Often our communications contain some strong emotional components. Our spoken words usually represent our thoughts and follow the rules of logic. Our nonverbal behavior often represents our emotional message. Think about popular songs. The lyrics carry a message, and the melody and rhythm create the hard-to-define aspect we think of as "the mood."

The verbal part of our communication is the message we intend to send. The nonverbal part is the message we inadvertently present. When we are aware of the power of our verbal and nonverbal messages, we can deliberately control both aspects so that the total communication is consistent, as intended.

Here are some ways that messages may be modified, clarified or entirely changed by the accompanying nonverbal behavior. Imagine someone saying:

"I have a message for you that is very important and I'm going to tell it to you now."

If this is the verbal message, then it can be sent most effectively by making sure the nonverbal message supports its clarity. If the speaker is unaware, nonverbal behaviors can detract

from the effectiveness of the intended communication.
- ☐ The vocal accompaniment can be unemotional, flat or neutral —a monotone with no variation in pitch, rhythm or pace.
- ☐ Vocal subverbal noises may not support the rest of the verbal message - sighing, yawning, halting "uhs."
- ☐ Physical behaviors may also distract the listener from the message - clothing, facial expression, eye contact, body movements.

Delivering an important verbal message without contradictory distractions can and must be a conscious performance. When a message is critically important, the delivery is likely to convey tension and concern. The expression of emotion through behaviors of tension and concern gives the listener a heightened message of importance that mere words can't convey. By maintaining emotional control, some persons are able to plan their nonverbal communication as well as they plan their verbal communication to send exactly what they want the listener to receive.

Now consider the message:

"I want you to check with me first before you make plans for us."

The statement could be a direction, a request, or a demand. The statement could even be a suggestion, in that it is capable of being restated as, "If you make plans that concern me, then let me know about them." The complete meaning as received by a listener will probably be determined by the nonverbal behavior that accompanies the speaking.

In other words, our total being communicates to and with others. Communication may be divided into three parts: *verbal behavior, vocal behavior,* and *physical appearance and behavior.*

We are most interested in the two nonverbal parts that contribute to the messages that we send, and what their implications are with regard to intimacy and control.

1. *Vocal behavior* includes volume, tone of voice, voice patterns, and also random vocalizing such as humming, whistling, singing, coughing, sighing, moaning, and grunting. Vocal behavior accompanies verbal behavior, and may intentionally or unintentionally contradict the verbal message, as in the case of a compliment expressed in a sarcastic tone of voice or with exaggerated mocking tones. From tone of voice and volume, emotional states are often inferred, such as secrecy, confidentiality and upset. Along with the "noises" of vocalizing, silence also communicates, though its message is not always clear. Vocal sounds tend to clarify, obscure or reinforce the verbal message.

We all are aware that there are sounds which are not quite words, that can be used to communicate agreement, disagreement, surprise, fear and other messages. Some of these are "uh oh," "ah ah!", "mm hmm." Some of these "sound words" or "vocal words" are meaningful because they actually reinforce the verbal message, physical behavior or both.

It is well known that some men and women have an extraordinary effect when they speak to individuals or to large groups of people. This is probably so because their vocal behavior *powerfully* complements and reinforces their verbal message.

2. *Physical appearance* is often the only consciously planned component of nonverbal behavior. Both the casual and the sloppy look may be carefully prearranged to send a particular message. Much information is inferred from physical appearance, and receivers are often influenced by stereotypes (e.g. social class, economic level, degree of refinement, age, political stance, etc.). Dressing in uniforms and costumes are deliberate strategies to send a message or create an impression that will influence others.

3. *Physical behavior* includes facial expression, eye contact, reaching out to touch, body movement and actions related to "territory" or personal distance between persons.

Facial expression is complex, and may give away or be a deliberate disguise to hide personal feelings. Facial expression may provide the most visible clue to the actual meaning of the verbal message because the face is usually the center of visual focus. Smiling, sneering, frowning, eyebrows raised, and mouth agape are all facial expressions that can affect the message intended and/or received. Some of these facial expressions and their meanings have made their way into our idiomatic language, and cliches, such as "keeping a stiff upper lip" or "gritting your teeth," and "tongue in cheek."

Eye contact is in a class all its own, because it is so powerful, and has many possible meanings or interpretations such as "I want you," "Come over here," "Hello," "I'm ok, you're ok," and "You're stupid." Lack of eye contact also has meaning, such as shyness, fear, anger, insecurity, or unwillingness to acknowledge a person. Many cultures see the eyes as the "windows of the soul," and thus staring into another's eyes can usually assure the truth of communication.

Body movements are countless. They may range from foot tapping and hand gestures to actual contact like hugging and kissing. They include body posture and walking style. In fact, so many are constantly occurring that listing them would be a complicated and perhaps meaningless task.

Territory and personal space behaviors include actions that convey feelings people have about the space directly around their bodies, as well as about the area they occupy for work or some other daily activity. How physically close you get or allow another person to be, and what behaviors of others you can accept comfortably in your office or your home are examples. Distance behaviors may depend on gender, the quality or closeness of your relationship with that person, the reason for your meeting, the time of day, the presence of other people, and so on. Acceptable behavior of others who are physically near you or in your home depend on personal limits and expectations that you have developed over your lifetime related

to your person and your property. Incidentally, within your home, your physical behavior and the arrangements of possessions send messages to others about your openness, formality and control.

Touch has potential to add emphasis and personal power to communication. Touching behavior may be conscious or unconscious, but either way it tends to strengthen or detract from the verbal message. The risk in touching may be that by violating the other's personal space, the entire message you intended to send may be lost. That person to whom you had been speaking cordially, though standing close to you, may *not* have wanted to be touched. Perhaps as young children we enjoyed a wide variety of touching. As we grew up, we learned to erect barriers to protect ourselves from pain and to prevent unwelcome direct physical contact with other people.

Recent research on verbal intimacy suggests that the extreme ends of the intimacy scale are easily and consensually identified by people. Most people understand and act on the messages of nonverbal intimacy or distance which their culture promotes. Additional research on nonverbal behaviors suggests that the most extreme behaviors of the intimacy scale are clear to people but the more subtle acts may be confusing. For this reason, the Nonverbal Intimacy Behavior Scale does not define a continuum of categories, but rather presents behaviors at the extremes of low and high intimacy.

The nonverbal control scale is similar to the nonverbal intimacy scale in that it identifies behaviors at the extremes. The issues raised by nonverbal behaviors have implications that are serious for relationships. They seem to fall into two conditions for our consideration:

1. *The message is totally nonverbal.* To some extent this appears to be a rare condition. People who share a relationship usually talk to one another, so it is somewhat unrealistic to think of nonverbal behaviors in isolation from verbal. However, there are situations that may be free of talking, and then

the nonverbal messages by themselves are of prime importance. These situations may include eating, reading, watching TV or any other activity that can be conducted alone yet in the presence of others. Other examples include situations in which people have visual contact but do not talk because of distance or distraction.

2. *Talking is going on and nonverbal messages are also being sent.* This situation occurs most of the time. Even talking on the phone cannot eliminate the nonverbal messages since tone, volume and pacing of verbal messages are really nonverbal clues to the meaning of the message. Nonverbal communication behaviors are important because they often provide the essential emotional definition of the verbal message.

Research through the years has indicated that nonverbal behaviors communicate a large part of most messages. Once we accept this reality, we must face the fact that our skill at decoding nonverbal messages are not nearly as developed as our ability to understand verbal messages.

Results of another research study suggest that restrictions placed on a small group's verbal or nonverbal behavior inhibit the development of group harmony. This effect is frequently seen in traditional classroom settings.

Similarly, in situations where verbal expression is accepted and nonverbal behavior is restricted (for example, when children dine with adults in a formal setting), verbal expressiveness will be limited by uneasy nonverbal behavior. This supports what common sense would predict. When life situations require restricted verbal or nonverbal communication, social development is inhibited.

SELF-INTIMACY AND SELF-CONTROL

"Self control" is usually considered an admirable trait and in most situations a necessity. But suppose that I over-control

or even suppress my actions for years because of social pressures and family responsibilities. At the same time my feelings are in disorder. I have suppressed them for so long that they are just about forgotten. Then one day, seemingly without warning, I explode in a rage or fall deeply into an isolating depression. Are these extreme actions admirable or necessary? Is it not more admirable and more necessary that feelings be recognized and accepted, so that appropriate actions may be taken as emotions are experienced? If I choose to live in the moment, my actions may not please those around me, but at least they will not result in extreme and problematic future upheavals. The point is that it is useful to think of self control as body-mind synergy rather than as one part of you taking over and making another part do something.

The concept of "self-intimacy" refers also to that synergy of various parts of our self, especially our thoughts and feelings. It is a matter of inner awareness. First let's think about how they relate to each other. Self-intimacy and self-control are related in that they both require *knowledge* of one's self. Knowing our thoughts, feelings and actions leads to wholeness and integration: being in touch with our selves. This knowledge helps us focus energy, be organized, make decisions and take action. Think of it in terms of a simple equation:

Intimacy with myself = Knowledge of myself + Control of myself

This self knowledge includes both feelings and perceptions I have about myself and the things I do. This knowledge map leads to *harmony* among my thinking, feeling and actions. Thus it is not surprising that self knowledge is so crucial to intimacy and control. How do we gain access to this important knowledge? Well, most of it simply comes naturally to each of us. Our most important behavior to assure access is careful listening and attention to our thoughts, our talk, our feelings, and our actions. Keeping a diary or journal of our thoughts,

feelings and reactions can help us be in touch with ourselves.

Paying attention to what others say to and about us is very important as well. Obtaining this self knowledge through the perceptions of others usually helps us feel more "whole" (intimate with ourselves) and "able" (in control of ourselves).

Some recent pilot research supports the idea that self-intimacy, intimacy with others, self-control, and control with others are all directly related. Positive attitudes toward self-intimacy, close relations with others, feeling in control of one's self and wanting to share control in relationships with others appear to cluster together. That is, if a person values one or more of these attributes, (s)he is likely to rank the others highly as well. This relationship among attitudes of intimacy and control appears to hold as well for people whose attitudes fall at the negative end of the scales, so that a person who has great resistance to close relationships with others, for example, is also likely to devalue being in touch with his/her inner self, experience a low level of self-control and want someone to be in control of his/her interpersonal relationships.

How does a positive relation between control and intimacy start? Think of it as starting *inside yourself.* You are aware of yourself, and have the tools and skills to increase your self-awareness. If you can accept yourself, you usually feel secure: in good control of yourself and emotionally receptive. Remember that "in good control" means having the freedom to choose from a self-determined range of behaviors. Emotional receptivity refers to a state of openness to experience feelings anywhere along an emotional range from anger to joy (rather than numbness or other unclear feeling). This inner condition can be thought of as heightened self-knowledge which is noticebly expressed in your talk and nonverbal behavior, much as other favorable inner conditions like happiness, confidence or good ideas readily show in your eyes.

Other people naturally respond favorably to you when you exhibit this condition. Even showing anger (rather than trying

to hide it) can help create a favorable impression. Appropriate verbal and nonverbal expression of anger can reflect awareness, confidence and an acceptance of mutual control and direct expression of feeling. Others sense that they are being approached by an open, sensitive and accepting person. Being around a person who can effectively express a full range of emotions can help others safely move toward their own greater self knowledge.

Suppose you are *not* very aware or accepting of yourself. You are then likely to be insecure: victimized by circumstances, disorganized, and perhaps emotionally cold, numb, or anxious. Victimized or disorganized people are easily dictated to and rightfully feel out of control. *Emotional coldness, numbness, or anxiety usually results when feelings have been suppressed, disregarded or disguised.* This inner condition may be thought of as a lack of self knowldge and self acceptance.

This inner condition may appear as pretense, criticism, judgment/evaluation of others, negative reactions, and other indirect expressions of feelings.

The insecure person may attempt to establish control through aggression or defensiveness. The other person(s) in the situation may tend to counter-attack in words or with gestures and other body expressions. Under these threatening conditions, low personal awareness and acceptance will limit the possibility for learning much more about one's self or the other(s).

We might say, overall, that awareness and acceptance of ourselves, and harmony of thought, feeling and action are essential ingredients in the development of high intimacy with others and mutual control. Experiencing high self intimacy and self control makes us naturally conscious of our connections with others. This consciousness leads the way to sensitivity with regard to others. It is convenient and practical for us to start with ourselves, and to assume responsibility for our own attitudes and behaviors. The focus here is on greater self

awareness and acceptance—greater intellectual and emotional self knowledge leading to better relations with others!

PEDESTAL THEORY ANALYSIS OF INTIMACY & CONTROL

Intimacy Category

1. Nonverbal Attraction No conversation,
Pity the poor slob. Superior. Other not as "good." Someone I can get. Not much risk in initiating., Fantasy - "Pie in the sky." They're too good for me. I have no chance. Too much risk of rejection,, Person/group reachable. I can risk initiation. I might be afraid,, but I'm as good as (s)he is., This person or group is reachable. I can risk initiation. I might be afraid,, but I am as good as he/she is.

2. Small Talk,
Pomposity —I'll impress themwith knowledge or experience *or* I really have nothing to waste on them., I'm dull,, don't know what to talk about; I'm uncomfortable;I'll act big or act nervous; or talk about the weather., Common/mutual interests; searching for and finding topics of intellectual conversation.

3. People in General,
People "should." My orientation is the only correct one., I'm insecure or unsure about what I believe. I may be wrong., Clear. I'm clear about my beliefs and I'm open to yours.

4. Individual Experience Outside the Relationship,
Bragging - self aggrandizement or underplay and patronizing., Reluctant to share faults & disappointments phony self aggrandizement to coverup., Honest exchange of experiences and common agenda.

5. Coversation About Others Not Present
Judgmental statements & opinions as though one is superior., Concern over feelings,, opinions,, judgments of others as thu-

ough they may reject., Matter of fact discussion of others as if they were present.

6. Shared Experience Past or Future,
Sharing of future hopes as definite plans., Subtle, indirect sharing of hopes, as if undeserving of achievement., Honest mutual sharing of hopes and concerns.

7. Individual Experience Feeling/Reaction,
Magnanimous or grandiose sharing or description of feelings. Manipulative or feigned sensitivity., Reluctant to share feelings or emotional reactions. Embarrassed. Timid. Ashamed, Honest sharing of emotion on both sides w/o fear of being taken advantage of.

8. Indirect Expression of Feeling,
Shoulds & other judgments about other(s) present. How they should behave or be., Insecure testing of how the other(s) might feel w/o stating one's own feelings., Bantering,, easy commentary on each other's behaviors,, qualities & feelings about each other.

9. Description of Shared Experience,
Judgment,, blaming,, attack,, or parental approving., Defensiveness,, as victim or attack & quick withdrawal., Feedback. Honest behavioral description w/o fear of aggression or rejection.

10. Direct Expression of Feeling,
No risk patronizing or overwhelming attack. Blaming & controlling., Defensiveness. Whining. Acting the part of the victom or insecure admirer., Sharing of honest feelings with intimate and honest agenda.

Control Category,

1. No Conversation,
Pity the poor slob. Superior. Other not as "good." Someone I

can beat. Not much risk., Fantasy-"Pie in the sky." He/She/They're too good for me. I have no chance. Great risk of defeat., This person or group is reachable. I can risk initiation.. I might be afraid,, but I'm as good as he/she is.

2. Negative Reaction,
Negative judgment. "That was a stupid thing to do!" "What kind of job is that?" Belittling statement toward other person., Tentative negative judgment. "Well,, I guess that was okay,, umh, maybe not." Fear of retaliation., "I got angry when you did that." Direct expression of negative feeling as a result of other's behavior.

3. Corrective Feedback,
"That was no way to do it. Why didn't you do it this way?" Definite negative assessment / past oriented. Offensive position., "Are you sure that's the way?" Tentative/ negative assessment/past oriented. Fear of retaliation. Defensive position., "This was my expectation. That is what you did. Next time will you do what I asked?" Formative feedback-chance to improve the future.

4. Direction,
"Do it my way without question." Authoritarian stance Aggressive., "Well,, what do you think of doing it this way?" Laissez faire stance. Passive., "These are the results I would like to achieve. This is the way I would like you to work. Any suggestions?" Assertive.

5. Suggestion or Advice, "
It's a shame that didn't work,, but there is only one way it will. Do it my way." Condescending stance., "Something went wrong ...an accident I guess. Maybe this will work." Tentative, symapthetic stance., "Here are a few alternatives. What do you think? I like this one." Definite empathetic stance.

6. Information,, Facts or Opinion,
"I'll tell you what the real facts are,, now that you're in trouble." Lecturing / condescending., "I think this way,, but

you may be right. I thought that might work." Tentative sharing of unsure information., "I accept your orientation to the problem. This is mine. Let's work together." Equal value of information.

7. Questions for Information,
"Where did you get your facts before you took that ludicrous action?" Negative judgment question., "I don't mean to question you,, but are you sure? Maybe it's okay." Tentative retreating question., "What is the procedure you used in the activity?" Definite,, clear request for information.

8. Questions for Clarification,
"Did you really believe that ridiculous strategy would work?" Negative judgment question., "Just for curiosity,, what does that mean? Oh,, never mind,, forgive me." Insecure question. Fear of seeming stupid., "What was the thinking behind your strategy,, in light of the overall plan?" Definite clear request for clarification.

9. Acknowledging,, Attending, Accepting,
"Not bad...not bad at all. Interesting viewpoint." Tentative acceptance, grudging acknowledgement., "Oh my! I never would have thought of that. How brilliant of you." Adoration, "apple-polishing.", "I understand what you did, and I appreciate both the effort and the results." Matter of fact acknowledgement.

10. Positive Reaction,
"How clever of you. That is reasonably good thinking. Better that I expected of you." Condescending / "left-handed" compliment, "Oh my! Thank you so much. You really saved me." Adoration,, "apple-polishing.", "I really like and appreciate what you have done for me and the group." Matter of fact appreciation.

Appendix 3

Cross Examination of Gary Heidnik

By Mr. Bolno:

Q   Mr. Heidnik, you are not married to Alberta Davidson, are you?

A   No, sir.

Q   You have never been married to Alberta Davidson, have you?

A   Are you saying Alberta or Angeanette?

Q   Yes, Alberta.

A   No,

Q   You don't have any devices in your apartment for the use of artificial insemination, do you?

A   No.

Q   You knew that Angeanette was Alberta's sister; isn't that correct?

A Yes.

Q Weren't you also aware that Alberta had been a resident of Sealingsgrove Institution prior to May 7th; were you aware that — strike the question.
Prior to May 7th, were you aware that Alberta had been a resident of the Sealingsgrove Institution for twenty years?

A Yes, sir. I don't know about the twenty years at the time.

Were you aware that Alberta had been a resident at the institution because she was mentally retarded; is that right?

A No, sir.

Now, you knew Angeanette; is that right?

A Yes, sir.

And you knew that Angeanette was retarded; isn't that correct?

A I knew she has learning difficulties.

Well, weren't you aware that she had trouble learning the designation of coins?

A I think one of the smartest men I know can't read.

That's not the question; were you aware that Angeanette had trouble learning the designation of coins?

A Yes, sir.

And didn't you in fact try to teach her what different coins were?

A Yes, sir.

And did you in fact try to teach her what they were in fact worth?

A Not worth, no?

Q Just what they were?

A Think so, yeah.

Q Was Angeanette aware what the coins were worth?

A Well, she went to the store if that's what you mean.

Q Did you trust her to make correct change?

A No, I don't think she made the correct change. The guy in the store, she would give — he would give her money.

Q And you would trust the people in the store to be honest with her; is that right?

A Yes, sir.

Q Now, you went to the Sealingsgrove Institution with Angeanette; isn't that right?

A Yes, sir.

Q And when you went there you met Mrs. Bolig who was the receptionist?

A Well, I didn't know what her name was, but I did meet a receptionist.

Q You had seen her?

A Yes, but at the time I didn't know what her name was.

Q You filled in the pass to take Alberta out?

A Yes, sir.

Q Isn't that because Angeanette can't read or write?

A She asked me to.

Q Can Angeanette read and write?

A No, sir — she can, but to a very limited extent.

Q And when you filled in that pass, you had a conversation with Mrs. Bolig about vacation; isn't that correct?

A Yes, sir.

Q And Mrs. Bolig told you that she could not approve the vacation; is that correct?

A No, it is not correct.

Q Did she tell you she could approve the vacation herself?

A I never asked the question that way to her.

Q Did you ask what procedure you would have to go through to have vacation for Alberta?

A Something to that effect.

Q Didn't she explain to you that it would have to be approved by her unit supervisor?

A No she did not.

Q What did she tell you then?

A All that had to be done was for them to be notified.

Q They had to be notified?

A Yes.

Q MR. BOLNO: Can I see C-1? You filled out C-1; isn't that right?

A Filled out?

Q C-1.

A What's C-1.

Q That's the pass from Sealingsgrove for Alberta?

A Part of it.

Q After you filled out this pass, you had to take it with you to pick up Alberta, didn't you?

A I think, I'm not sure about that part of the procedure.

Q Well, don't you recollect Alberta could not be released from her unit unless you showed them a pass?

A No, I don't remember that part.

Q You don't recollect that? Did you read this pass?

A Most of it.

Q You saw that this pass was approved for a ride; is that correct?

A Say that again.

Q You saw that it was circled on this pass that you were approved to take Alberta out for a ride; isn't that right?

A I don't remember that.

Q Do you see — Mr. Bolno: May the witness be shown —

A The Defendant: I remember seeing that it was circled there, and I remember having, you know said that —

Q On the same line that the word "ride" appears, there are other designations?

A Yes, sir.

Q What are the other designations?

A "A day out; ride; visit; R. vacation; long vacation or L. vacation."

Q The only one that is circled is the "ride" isn't that correct?

A Yes, sir.

Q Are there times that are also indicated on that pass?

A   Yes, sir.

Q   And what are the times that are indicated on the pass?

A   "12: 3, and" —

Q   "12: 3?

A   Yeah, if you want to be exact.

Q   What is that supposed to mean to you?

A   I suppose to twelve thirty.

Q   That's the time you arrived at Sealingsgrove?

A   Yes, sir.

Q   What's the other time indicated on the pass?

A   Four with a line, zero, zero; I assume that's four o'clock.

Q   In the afternoon?

A   Right.

Q   That clearly was a pass to take Alberta out for a ride from twelve thirty to 4:00 P.M.?

A   Yes, sir.

Q   You were aware of that; isn't that correct?

A   Then?

Q   Then.

A   I don't remember the exact time or anything like that. When we were there, we were just told we are to take her out for the day — for a couple of hours, I am sorry.

Q   Without remembering the exact time, were you aware that you had received a pass to take Alberta out for a ride for some few hours in the afternoon?

A Yes, sir.

Q And you were also aware that you had not received a pass to take Alberta out for vacation; isn't that correct?

A There could be some doubt in my mind.

Q Mr, Heidnik, do you have any doubt that you did not receive a pass to take Alberta out for a vacation?
Mr. Pressman: May it please the Court, I object to this line of questioning.
The Court: Overruled.
Mr. Pressman: May I state my reason, your Honor? It would appear on the surface as to what your Honor thinks this whole line of questioning addresses as to what Gary Heidnik was granted. Gary Heidnik was not granted anything. Angeanette was granted a pass to take her sister out.
Mr. Bolno; Your Honor, I object to these speeches. We are on cross-examination.
The Court: The Commonwealth is sustained. The defense is overruled.

Q Were you aware that you had not received a pass which would allow you to take Alberta—
The Court: All right, may it please counsel, if counsel finds the *Legal Intelligencer* of this morning to be so important, we will take a recess.
Mr. Pressman: Are you talking about Mr. Bulkin?
Mr. Bulkin: I am sorry your Honor.
Mr. Bolno: I'll restate the question if I may, your Honor.

Q Mr, Heidnik, were you aware when you received that pass that we are talking about, that that pass did not allow you to take Alberta out for vacation?

A Well, you know, this pass here says Angeanette Davidson, and that's who the pass was granted to, sir.

Q Were you aware that the pass did not allow you or Angeanette Davidson to anyone to take Alberta out for vacation?

A No, I was not.

Q You were not aware of that?

A No, sir.

Q. Well, you picked Alberta up; is that correct?

A Yes, sir.

Q And when you picked Alberta up, did she take a suitcase with her?

A No suitcase, no, sir.

Q Did she take a change of underwear with her?

A Well, she had a pocketbook with her. I don't know what she had in it.

Q Did she take another pair of pants or a skirt or a dress or any other article of clothing other than what she was wearing?

A I am not sure, but I don't believe so, no, sir.

Q Did she take a coat with her?

A No, sir.

Q She didn't — did she take a tooth brush with her?

A I don't know.

Q Did she take any medication with her?

A She may have had these things in her pocketbook, I don't know.

Q Were you aware, Mr. Heidnik, that when she left with you that day that she needed to take drugs for her con-

dition of anemia?

A   No, I was not.

Q   Did you make any inquiry as to whether or not she needed to take any medication with her?
Mr. Pressmen: I am going to object to this line of questioning.
The Court: Overruled and no speech.
The Defendant: I wasn't really my concern. It was Alberta's sister.

Q   Were you aware of the fact that Alberta Davidson was suffering from anemia and if she had gone for an extended period without taking specific drugs for the treatment of that disease, that it could be fatal to her?
Mr. Pressmen: Objection.
The Court: Overruled.
The Defendant: If I remember my nursing training, anemia is a chronic disease. It's not fatal. It seldom is fatal if it is real.

Q   Were you aware, Mr. Heidnik — please answer my question this time — that Alberta Davidson was suffering from anemia; that a certain drug was prescribed for that treatment, and that if she went for an extended period of time without that drug, that it could be fatal to her?

A   At this time?

Q   At that time.

A   No, sir.

Q   Now, Mr. Heidnik, when you picked Alberta Davidson up, did she appear to you that she was coming with you prepared to go on a week and a half vacation?

A   No. sir, she was coming you know?

Q Did she appear to you that she was coming with you prepared to go out for a ride for a few hours' duration?

A More than likely, yes, sir.

Q And as a matter of fact, after you had gone out to eat, you were at that point ready to bring her back; isn't that correct?

A After the ice cream, yes, sir.

Q And that was because you were aware of the fact that she was only allowed to have left Sealingsgrove for a ride on that occasion; isn't that correct?
Mr. Pressman: Objection.
The Court: Overruled
The Defendant: It was more like I was on a limited time schedule. I had to be back in Philadelphia at a certain time to go back to work.

Q If you had to be back at a certain time to go to work and you believed that Alberta could have left and gone for a vacation, then you wouldn't have had to bring her back to Sealingsgrove; isn't that right?

A Try that once again.(Whereupon the Court Reporter read back the following:"Question: If you had to be back at a certain time to go to work and you believed that Alberta could have left and gone for a vacation, then you wouldn't have had to bring her back to Sealingsgrove; isn't that right?") THE DEFENDANT: Yes, sir.

Q And therefore, isn't it correct that the reason you were concerned about bringing her back to Sealingsgrove was because that's what you understood your duty to have been?

A Not necessarily.

Q Let's go back. You said that you took Alberta to a res-

taurant; is that correct?

A   Yes, sir.

Q   And when you went to the restaurant, were you issued menus to read?

A   Yes, sir.

Q   Was Alberta able to read her menu?

A   No, sir.

Q   How did in fact Alberta get to choose what she wanted to order?

A   I read the menu off to them and asked them what they wanted to eat.

Q   Did Alberta tell you what she wanted?

A   Yes, sir, meatloaf.

Q   What did she want?

A   Meatloaf.

Q   When the waitress came, who asked for the meatloaf?

A   I think it was her, but I am not sure.

Q   Did Alberta have money to pay for the meatloaf?

A   I don't know.

Q   You went to a store with Alberta in Philadelphia, didn't you?

A   Several times, yes, sir, and Angeanette.

Q   Did Alberta have money to pay for anything?

A   Angeanette always told me to buy her—buy her that.

Q   Did you ever see Alberta handle money in your presence?

A Not really, no.

Q Well, what do you mean by "Not really, no;" did you ever see her handle money?

A Well, like she would go to the store, right. You would give her a dollar, and she would put it in her pocketbook and get a quart of milk for me, something like that.

Q Did you ever send her with a shopping list?

A No. The store on the corner is just a little store, really don't have much.

Q You knew Sealingsgrove was a mental institution, didn't you?

A No, sir.

Q Well, didn't you tell Mr. Pressman on direct examination that you knew Sealingsgrove was a mental institution?

A I said that it was some kind of institution, like a boarding school. I think I said boarding school or boarding home or —

Q Or mental institution?

A That doesn't mean that I knew what it was.

Q My question is: Mr. Heidnik, isn't it correct that you told Mr. Pressman on your direct examination that Sealingsgrove was a mental institution?

A I said I wasn't sure, and I listed three possibilities.

Q You were aware that Alberta had been institutionalized for twenty years; isn't that correct?

A I became aware of it sometime. I don't remember when; before or after this day.

Q   Well, you told us earlier in my examination of you that you were aware of that before May 7th, 1978; isn't that correct?

A   I don't remember that.
Mr. Bolno: Well, may the record be read back to that point, Mr. Heidnik's answer to that question?
The Court: Read it back.
Mr. Bolno: Your Honor, I'll withdraw the request of Mr. Venturo at this point.

Q   Why did you think Alberta Davidson had been institutionalized for a period of twenty years?

A   You know, I wasn't sure if it was a school, maybe a boarding home, a large boarding home, mental institution.

Q   Well, you observed Alberta Davidson when you picked her up at Sealingsgrove?

A   Yes, sir

Q   You observed her when you went out and had lunch with her?

A   Yes, sir.

Q   You observed that she couldn't read; isn't that correct?

A   Yes, sir.

Q   You observed her appearance; isn't that right?

A   Yes, sir.

Q   Is there anything out of the ordinary about her appearance?

A   As I said, it looked like benign neglect. Her hands were very chapped and had this dry skin on them.

Q   When you say "benign neglect," is it correct that you

are assuming that she needed someone to care for her; is that correct?

A It might have been her that just didn't care.

Q You told Mr. Pressman on direct examination that it appeared to you that the institution had benignly neglected her; isn't that correct, didn't you tell that to—

A Well, if she obviously needed some help —

Q And what about — what was it that made you conclude that she obviously needed some help?

A Her hair; her hands. She was — I don't remember when, but she explained that the condition of her hands resulted from some job she had there working with furniture and some kind of chemical to that effect.

Q So she didn't appear capable herself then of arranging her hair so it wouldn't look out of the ordinary?
Mr. Pressman: Objection.
The Court: Sustained.

Q So then it was your assumption, Mr. Heidnik, on May 7th, 1978, that when Alberta appeared to have been treated with benign neglect, that she was in need of being taken care of; isn't that correct"

A No, not necessarily.

Q Would you explain your answer.

A Like the job that she was on, now, you know, she is working on a job. It seems funny they are supposed to care, that they would put her in a job situation that was so harmful to her.

Q Well, then you knew, did you not, that she was in a situation where somebody needed to care for her; you just said that you knew that.

Mr. Pressman: Objection.
The Court: Overruled.
The Defendant: I think I said too —

Q Would you answer my question; did you know then that she was in a situation where somebody needed to care for her?

A Not entirely, no. The point I am trying to make —
Mr. Pressman: No.

Q You can explain your answer, Mr. Heidnik; what point are you trying to make?

A That by having this type work and the condition of her hands, you know, it's — it could be maybe like abuse.

Q So you determined that the institution was abusing her; is that correct?

A No, I did not.

Q You thought that you would take care, better care, of her; is that correct?

A Not me; Angeanette.

Q Well, you know that Angeanette isn't capable of taking care of herself entirely, don't you?

A She takes pretty good care of herself and me.

Q She can't count, can she?

A So?

Q She can't read, can she?

A Yes, she can, to a limited extent.

Q Can she write?

A To a limited extent.

Q Could she write well enough to fill out that pass?

A No.

Q Well, you don't believe that Angeanette —

A I think what she could have done, you know, wrote like her sister's name. She could have wrote her name and address, but I don't think she knew what like a Visitor's Introduction, she wouldn't have been able to read that or resident's name. She wouldn't know what that was.

Q So you don't believe that Angeanette was fully capable of taking care of herself; isn't that so?
Mr. Pressman: Objection.
The Court: Overruled.
The Defendant: Not being able to read doesn't mean that you can't take care of yourself.

Q Well, would you believe, knowing Angeanette capable of taking care of herself, that she could go into a strange store and be reasonably certain that she wouldn't lose her money or be taken advantage?

A You can never be sure of that. Somebody might snatch her pocketbook or, you know, counting was a problem with her.

Q Could you be sure that Angeanette, if she was in a strange part of the city would be able to find her way home by public transportation?

A Sure.

Q You feel sure of that?

A Yes, sir. Angeanette had several jobs before I met her in the sheltered workshop, but she did have her jobs.

Q How does that make you sure that Angeanette would be able to find her way home from a strange part of the city?

A She got there, didn't she?

Q That's your answer?

A I am not sure I am interpreting your question right.

Q I think my question is simple: How could you be sure that Angeanette, by public transportation, could find her way home from a strange part of the city?

A How could I be sure? I can't think of any instances off-hand, but she has. I can't think of specific instances where she went, but she has done it. I think she just asked the bus driver or something to that effect. I know when I had problems, that's what I would do.

Q Now, you have said that Angeanette was slow; is that correct?

A I don't remember if I said that, but she was a little slow, yes, sir.

Q And you observed Alberta when you took her out on this pass during the afternoon of May 7th, 1978; isn't that correct?

A Yes, sir.

Q And you observed that she couldn't read?

A Yes, sir.

Q You observed her general demeanor: isn't that right?

A What's demeanor mean?

Q The way she acted.

A Yes, sir.

Q And did you observe her as far as her social ability is concerned, the way people act towards one another?

A Pretty much so.

Q Did she seem to act the way a thirty-four year old woman would act?

A No.

Q Well, how did she act differently than how you would think a thirty-four year old woman would act?

A Well, she — I guess the best words are, she seemed a little slow, but she seemed functional. I mean, when you read the menu, she knew what she wanted.

Q Well, she was able — she knew what meatloaf was; isn't that right?

A Yes, sir.

Q Now, Mr. Heidnik, you are a person who has a background of some education; isn't that correct?

A Yes, sir.

Q You have told us about what education you had; isn't that right?

A Yes, sir.

Q Now, putting all things together, knowing that Alberta was institutionalized for twenty years, knowing that she appeared a little odd, knowing that she was slow, did you have any conclusion as to why Alberta had been institutionalized at Sealingsgrove?
Mr. Pressman: Objection.
The Court: Overruled.
The Witness: Could be — I couldn't say for sure, really.

Q What was your conclusion; I know you can't say for sure.

A I made no conclusion. There are various possibilities, you know.

Q Let's go on, Mr. Heidnik. On May 8th you received a

phone call from Ella Neverington (phonetic) from the Sealingsgrove Institution?

A May 8th would be Monday?

Q Well, it would be the day — did you take Alberta out on a Sunday?

A Right.

Q That would be Monday then.

A To tell you the truth, I don't remember. Over a period of a couple of days, we made and received phone calls. I don't remember the contents of each phone call and which phone and who I talked to or who Angeanette or Alberta talked to.

Q On May 8th, 1978, didn't you receive a phone call from some person at the Sealingsgrove Institution —

A I don't remember.

Q I haven't finished my question.— in which you indicated that you would take Alberta and put her on a bus leaving from Philadelphia and that the bus would arrive in Harrisburg; didn't you tell some person at Sealingsgrove on May 8th?

A I told somebody that. I don't remember on which date I told them.

Q Was it within a day or two after you had taken Alberta from the Sealingsgrove Institution?

A I know I told them a couple of times. I don't know which days exactly when I told them.

Q Do you recall whether it was in a day or two, not the precise day or two, when you had taken Alberta from Sealingsgrove?

A No, I don't.

Q You don't know the phone call —

A Not exactly, no. You are asking me for one specific phone call. No, I don't remember specifically. I do remember having told them that I would put her on a bus and send her back.

Q Now, as a matter of fact, you didn't do that, did you?

A No, sir.

Q So you lied to those people when you said you were going to do that; isn't that correct?

A Not exactly when I told them that I had intended to do that.

Q Did you ever call them back and tell them that you would not do that?

A No, sir, I did not.

Q So then if you did not lie, you deceived them; isn't that correct?
Mr. Pressman: Objection.
The Court: Overruled.
The Defendant: I am not sure I made the distinction on that.

Q Mr. Heidnik, you did not call and tell them that you were not going to put Alberta on the bus; isn't that correct?

A Yes, sir.

Q You did not clear up a misimpression; isn't that correct?

A Yes, sir.

Q Do you recall receiving phone calls from Sealingsgrove in which it was pointed out to you that you had no authority to have Alberta with you?

A I remember there were numerous calls, and they wanted, among other things, to talk to Alberta and Angeanette, and they did.

Q Are you telling us that someone from Sealingsgrove talked to Alberta?

A Yes, sir, I certainly am.

Q Well, answer my question —

A Several times.

Q Were you not informed by telephone on numerous occasions that you did not have the authority to keep Alberta in your apartment?

A I wasn't keeping her there. In effect, she was Anjeannette's sister. Angeanette wanted her to stay.

Q Mr. Heidnik, were you not informed by telephone on many occasions that Alberta was not authorized to be out of that institution?

A I was, you know — yes.

Q Now, you met Sally Snauffer on May 16th, 1978 at Family Court; isn't that correct?

A Yes, sir.

Q And you told her on that date that the night before you had placed Alberta on a bus; isn't that correct?

A I don't remember saying the night before. I did tell her that I had placed her on a bus, though.

Q You had not placed Alberta on a bus at any time; isn't that correct?

A Yes, sir.

Q That was a lie; is that not correct?

A Yes, sir.

Q It was your intention to hide Alberta at that time; isn't that correct?

A Alberta did not want to go back, and Angeanette did not want me to send her back.

Q Mr. Heidnik, what was the purpose of your lying to Sally Snauffer on May 16th, 1978?

A To satisfy Angeanette.

Q By hiding Alberta Davidson?

A Yes, sir.

Q What was your purpose of taking Alberta to a storage bin on May 17th, 1978?

A Alberta was afraid they were going to force her to go back. She did not want to go back, and Angeanette didn't want me to let them take her.

Q So you had hid Alberta; isn't that correct?

A Angeanette and I hid her, yes, sir.

Q You took Sally Snauffer back to your apartment on May 16th, 1978; isn't that correct?

A I believe that was the date.

Q Did you tell Sally Snauffer that Alberta was at Jule's?

A No, sir, I did not.

Q Why not?

A Because as I said again, Alberta did not want to go back. Angeanette did not want me to send her back, and Angeanette wanted me to try to hide her.

Q And it was your intention to hide her; is that not cor-

rect?

A Yes, sir.
The Court (to the defendant): Who is Jules?
The Defendant: It's not Jules. It's Jule Centron (phonetic). She is a nurse that I had known about ten years ago. She is about fifty years old now, I believe, and she was a friend.
The Court: When did you take Alberta to Jule?
The Defendant: The day of the Family Court hearing — the night before, I took her there the night before, and she stayed there all day that we were in the hearing, and she stayed there that night, and I picked her up when I came off from work. I picked her up when I came off from work.
The Court: Did you work?
The Defendant: No, sir.
The Court: Who else lived at that house or apartment besides Jule?
The Defendant: There was Jule. She had two sons. One is something like twenty or twenty-one years old, I believe; another one fourteen. She has a daughter; a granddaughter; there are several grandchildren that sort of come and go, plus occasionally they have overnight visitors. It's in North Philly.

Q Now, you have told us that you never told Audrey Davis to get your lubricating gel because it was time to break in Alberta?

A No, sir.

Q Are you also lying when you deny that?

A No, sir.

Q Didn't you tell Audrey Davis on an earlier date that Alberta was a virgin and it was time that she was broken in?

A   No, sir, I did not.

Q   You heard Audrey Davis testify that you left with Alberta early in the morning of the date of your Family Court hearing, the 16th of May; isn't that correct?

A   I don't remember her saying that.

Q   You don't recall her saying that?

A   No, sir.

Q   If she had testified to that fact, would you say that Audrey Davis was lying?

A   Say that again.

Q   If she had testified to that fact, would you say that Audrey Davis was lying?

A   Yes, sir.

Q   When you drove to the OB/GYN Clinic on May 15th, 1978, do you have any specific recollection about where Alberta was sitting?

A   She was sitting in the car by the door, and Angeanette was sitting in between.

Q   Do you say that because that's where Alberta normally sat?

A   Angeanette always liked to sit next to me.

Q   Do you say that because that's where Alberta normally sat?

A   I mean, yeah, that's where she normally sat.

Q   Do you have any specific recollections about where she was in the car on that particular ride?

A   The other side of Angeanette. And Audrey Davis, Miss Davis, was in the back seat.

Q Didn't you ask Miss Davis if she had gotten the lubricating gel on the way back from the clinic?

A No, sir, I did not.

Q You treated Mr. who?

A You mean who did I work for?

Q Yes.

A Mr. John Redmen.

Q And he is a private patient of yours?

A Yes, sir.

Q You told us that you take his temperature?

A On occasions.

Q In or around May 17, 1978, do you recall if Mr. Redmen was suffering from a fever?

A He developed a fever, but I don't think it was then. I think it was later he developed kidney complications for which he was transferred to Jefferson; but I don't think it was on that date. I think it was after.

Q How long prior to May 7, 1978 had you been treating Mr. Redmen?

A Prior to May 7th, I'd say over a year.

Q And had he developed a fever during the course of that year at any time, if you can recall?

A We didn't take — you know, like I was working nights, right. Usually, unless there is a critical situation, the day nurse would take the temperature. Occasionally I would, especially if I suspected something. Now, what was the question?

Q Have you ever treated him for a fever over the course

of the year prior to May 7th that you had been working there?

A Treat or take his temperature?

Q Were you ever aware that he had a fever during the year prior to May 7th?

A I think he had one in Jeff, but that was like a year ago. I think he had pneumonia when I first came on the case, if I remember right, among other things.

Q Was he treated with antibiotic drugs?

A I don't remember. You would have to ask the nurse at Jefferson. It would be in the records, I am sure.

Q When he got out of Jeff. —

A As an L.P.N. — I am not an R.N. When a patient is in the hospital, usually the R.N. are the ones that give the medication.

Q Not always?

A Not always, no, but usually in private duty situations. I varies from hospital to hospital.

Q Now, he was released from Jefferson after he suffered from pneumonia; is that correct?

A Yes, sir. He had other complications, too.

Q Did he come home with any medication?

A He had considerable medication at home, yes, sir.

Q And weren't some of those medications antibiotic medications?

A I don't know.

Q And wasn't it part of your duty to administer medications to Mr. Redmen when he was home?

A   I am trying to remember. I don't think that he got anything at nighttime. No he didn't get anything at nighttime, no, sir.

Q   You mean he wouldn't get any medication from eight o'clock at night until the next morning?

A   Yeah, yeah, wait a minute. He did get some medication for a kidney infection somewhere in there. You know, I really have to check the nurses' notes to bring this all into focus.

Q   As a matter of fact, Mr. Heidnik, for a long period of time through the dates of May 7th, 1978 up until the first week of June 1978 and starting a year prior to that, you did have access to antibiotic drugs through your work, didn't you?

A   Yes, sir.

Q   When you received your training as an L.P.N., part of that training was to learn about various diseases; isn't that correct?

A   Yes, sir.

Q   You learned about the diseases of gonorrhea during the course of your training; isn't that correct?

A   Yes, sir.

Q   As of May 17th, 1978 you were aware that gonorrhea was treated with antibiotic drugs, were you not?

A   Certainly.

Q   Penicillin was one of those drugs; aren't you aware of that?

A   I think so. There are several antibiotics if I remember right.

Q   You are aware of the fact that gonorrhea could be

treated by several antibiotic drugs, aren't you?

A Yes, sir.

Q And as a matter of fact, you had access to those drugs between May 7th and the first week in June, 1978; isn't that correct?

A He had antibiotics there. I don't believe he had penicillin. I don't remember the name of it, but he had some new, very expensive antibiotic. I think it started with a G that he was taking for prevention of kidney disease.

Q On the morning of the 17th, you testified that on a few occasions you heard knocks on the door but didn't go to the door; isn't that correct?

A Yes, sir.

Q You have also told us that both Angeanette and Alberta had access to that door; is that not correct?

A Yes, sir.

Q Do you have any knowledge at all as to why either Alberta or Angeanette didn't answer the door when there was knocks?

A Not specifically, but maybe they thought — they thought it was somebody banging on Miss Davis's door. You really can't distinguish.

Q Your common experience with Angeanette, if you didn't answer the door there some long period of knocks, would Angeanette answer the door?

A Not necessarily.

Q In other words, you would just go on and listen to the knocks; isn't that correct?

A You said Angeanette answered the door.

Q Now, you know that Angeanette was slow; isn't that correct?

A A little bit, yes, sir.

Q You knew that Angeanette couldn't count correctly; isn't that correct?

A Did you say count well?

Q Yes.

A Yes.

Q You knew she could only read to a limited extent?

A Yes.

Q You knew she could only write to a limited extent?

A Yes, sir.

Q You knew that Alberta was slow; isn't that correct?

A She seemed so, yes, sir.

Q Could you explain your answer that there would be no danger to Alberta as long as she was with Angeanette?

A Like, you know, I think you are trying to think Angeanette couldn't do anything. That's not true. She cooked for me and cleaned for me; washed my uniform; ironed it. If I needed something from the store, from the local store which was limited, if what they had, she would go to the store, stuff like this.

Q Mr. Heidnik, you are telling us that Angeanette served you in all little, small details in your life; isn't that correct?

A Say again.

Q She served you?

A   Served, no.

Q   She did for you?

A   She took care of me.

Q   But Mr. Heidnik, isn't it true that when to came to any important decision, that you made that decision for Angeanette?

A   No.

Q   Isn't it true, Mr. Heidnik, that Angeanette lied?

A   You don't know Angeanette very well.

Q   Isn't it true Mr. Heidnik, Angeanette relied on you to make important decisions for her?

A   You don't know Angeanette very well. If Angeanette wanted something, she had a way of making her wishes known.

Q   Now, you were present, Mr. Heidnik, when Angeanette came out of the storage closet on the 17th; isn't that correct?

A   Angeanette?

Q   When Alberta came out of the storage closet on the 17th.

A   I didn't see her come out at first, you know. I was standing there playing the pinball machine while they were going through the hallways searching. Then I heard someone say, "We found her." Then I went over there into the other section and stood in the entrance there.

Q   And you saw Alberta throw herself into the arms of Dr. Biggamin?

A   No, I did not.

Q Did you see Alberta throw herself into the arms of Sally Snauffer?

A No, I did not.

Q Did you see her in the arms of Sally Snauffer?

A I saw Miss Snauffer patting and hugging; didn't see Alberta going to her.

Q Didn't you hear Alberta telling Miss Snauffer that she wanted to return to the Sealingsgrove Institution?
Mr. Pressman: Objection.
The Court: Overruled.
The Defendant: After about five minutes of pleading and talking to her by Miss Snauffer, yes, sir.

Q And is it still your testimony that you heard — strike that. Is it still your testimony that you hid Alberta out because she herself did not want to return to the Sealingsgrove Institution?

A Angeanette and I hid her, and she, that is, Alberta, did not want to go back. I think she just succumbed to the pressures of Miss Snauffer and all the police officers. There were several policemen there also, and I think she was scared too.

Q Now, were you ever alone in the apartment with Alberta?

A I may have been without really knowing it. You know, like I work nights, right. I got some sleep on the job actually, and when I would come home, a lot of times I would have breakfast or go out and eat. Then I would go to bed, and I would close the door. The two, Angeanette and Alberta, would be out in the living room. Now, Angeanette may have gone to the store or something to that effect, but Alberta would thus be in the apartment with me, and I wouldn't have known

that.

Q Now, Angeanette took care of you, is that right; she did things for you?

A As a wife, yes, sir.

Q She would take your laundry out to be done?

A We didn't have any laundromats near us. You had to walk fifteen or twenty blocks. Usually if we take clothes to the laundromat, I would drive her there.

Q Were there laundry facilities in your building?

A No, sir.

Q Did she go to the store to purchase food?

A Yes, sir.

Q Did she go to the neighborhood drugstore to purchase?

A We don't have a neighborhood drugstore.

Q Did she ever go out for a walk on her own?

A Oh, yes — wait, are we talking about Angeanette or Alberta?

Q Angeanette.

A Right.

Q Did Angeanette have friends from the building?

A To a limited extent.

Q Wasn't she friendly with Audrey Davis?

A To a limited extent. Miss Davis kept telling her that she should leave me, among other things.

Q But Angeanette was still friendly?

A Yeah, but she didn't appreciate Miss Davis telling her.

Q As a matter of fact, during the course of Alberta's visit, didn't Angeanette visit Miss Davis?

A I believe they both went up there.

Q Didn't Angeanette visit Miss Davis by herself?

A She did on several occasions. I don't remember during the course of these events if it was during those times. You know, like in the morning sometimes I didn't always sleep in the morning. Like sometimes I would get my sleep in the afternoon. If they wanted to leave or do something like that, they were free to do it, and I would be in the bedroom, and I wouldn't be aware of it.

Q Mr. Heidnik, isn't it a fact that between May 7th and 17th there were numerous occasions when Angeanette left the apartment by herself; isn't that correct?

A No, I don't know that.

Q Mr. Heidnik, is it your testimony that every time that Angeanette left the apartment by herself, that you were locked in the bedroom and weren't aware of Alberta's presence?

A Say that again.

Q Is it your testimony that every time that Angeanette left the apartment by herself, that you were in the bedroom and you were not aware of Alberta's presence?

A Conceivable. Sometimes you are in the bedroom and you are not fully aware. I could hear Angeanette leaving.

Q And you could hear Alberta in the apartment; isn't that correct?

A Well, you know, you couldn't be sure who left.

Q Did you ever see Alberta in the apartment by herself one time between May 7th and May 17th, 1978?

A I am sure I probably did, but I don't remember specific instances.

Q So it is correct, Mr. Heidnik, that you were; you said you are sure that you were alone with Alberta, to your knowledge, in the apartment between May 7th and May 17th; isn't that correct?

A Say that again.

Q Mr. Heidnik, you have told us that you are sure that you did see Alberta alone in the apartment?

A I didn't see — oh, yeah.

Q So is it not correct that you are sure that you were alone in the apartment between May 7th and May 17th with Alberta?

A Not necessarily.
Mr. Bolno: I have no further questions.
The Defendant: See, I can't remember specific instances, but sometimes I would be like out in the hallway playing with the pinball machine or trying to fix the pinball machine, and she would be in the apartment, and the door would be open.

Q So that every time Angeanette left the apartment, Mr. Heidnik, you were not in the bedroom with the door closed; is that right?

A No, of course not.
Mr. Bolno: No further questions.
The Court: Any redirect?
Mr. Pressman: None, sir
The Court: You may step down.

Bibliography

Amidon, E.M., Amidon, M., Apsche, J.A., and Silverman. *The Intimacy Manual,* International Information Associates, Inc. Pennsylvania 1992.

Anstett, R.E. and Wood L. "The Patient Exhibiting Episodic Violet Behavior". *The Journal of Family Practice,* Vol. 16, No. 3: 605-609 (1983).

Axelrod, S., and Apsche, J.A. *The Effects of Punishment on Human Behavior.* Academic Press, New York (1983).

Britain, R. P. "The Sadistic Murderer." *Medical Science and the Law,* 1970, 10: 198-207.

Dietz, P.E. "Mass, Serial and Sensational Homicides." *Bulletin of the New York Academy of Medicine* (2d series), 62: 5: 447-490, June 1986

Dietz, P.E. "Sex Offenses: Behavioral Aspects." In *Kadish S.(ed): Encyclopedia of Crime Justice.* New York: Free Press, 1485-93, 1983.

Erseeff, G.S. and Wisniewski, E.M. "A Psychiatric Study of A Violent Mass Murderer." *Journal of Forensic Science.* 17 (1972).

Holmes, R.M. and DeBurger, J.E. "Profiles in Terror! The Serial Murderer," *Federal Probation,* Vol. 49, 1985, 29-34.

Levin, J. and Fox, J.E. *Mass Murder: America's Growing Menace.* Plenum, New York (1985).

Lewis, D.O., Moy, B.S., Jackson, L.D., Aaronson, R., Restifo, N. Serra, S. and Simos, A. "Biopsychosocial Characteristic of Children Who Later Murder: A Prospective Study." *American Journal of Psychiatry,* 142: 10, October 1985.

MacCulloch M.J., Snowden, P.., Wood, P.J.W., and Mills, H.E. "Sadistic Fantasy, Sadistic Behaviors and Offending." *British Journal of Psychiatry,* 1983, 143, 20-29.

Mac Donald, J.M. "The Threat to Kill," *American Journal of Psychiatry,* 120 (1963).

Norris, J. *Serial Killers: The Growing Menace.* Doubleday, New York (1988).

Rappapart, R.G. "The Serial and Mass Murderers: Patterns, Differentiation, Pathology." *American Journal of Forensic Psychiatry,* Vol IX, No. 1, 1988, 739.

Reinhardt, J.M. "Sex Perversions and Sex Crimes: A Psycholocultural Examination of the Causes, nature and criminal manifestations of sex perversions," *Police Science Series.* Springfield, IL: Charles C. Thomas, 1975.

Ressler, R.K., Burgess, A.W., and Douglas, J.E. *Sexual Homicide; Patterns and Motives.* Lexington Books, Massachusetts (1988).

Ressler, R.K. and Shachtman. *Whoever Fights Monsters.* St. Martins Press, New York, 1992

Ressler, R.K. *FBI Law Enforcement Bulletin,* 1985, 54 - 1043.

Skinner, B.F. *About Behaviorism.* Vintage Books, New York (1974).

Skinner, B.F. *Science and Human Behavior.* Macmillan Company, New York (1953).

Taylor, P.J. "Motives of Offending among Violent and Psychotic Men." *British Journal of Psychiatry* (1985), 147, 491-498.

Taylor, P.J. and Gunn, J. (1984) "Violence and Psychosis II - Effects of Psychiatric Diagnosis on Conviction and Sentencing of Offenders." *British Medical Journal,* 289, 9-12.

West, P.J., Roy, C. and Nicholas F.L. *Understanding Sexual*

Attacks, London: Heinemann, 1978.

Wolfgang, M.E. *Pattern of Homicide.* Philadelphia: University of Pennsylvania Press, 1958.

Wolfgang, M.E. and Terracuti, F. *The Subculture of Violence: Toward An Integrated Theory In Criminology.* 2nd. ed. Beverly Hills, California: Sage Publications, 1982.

Index

A

Amidon, Edmund	27
Aura phase	11
Autoeroticism	13

B

Baron Gilles	6
Behavior reinforcement	137
Bishop Heidnik aka Gary Heidnik	51
Brown, Tony	104

C

Characteristics, juvenile predictors	15
Control	12, 59, 77
Serial killing	114
Control after victim death	29
Corrective feedback	170
Crime spree killer	4
Custodial poisoners	4

D

Davidson, Alberta	39
Davidson, Angeanette	39
Pregnancy	44

Deitz, Park	3
Direction, instruction, command	171
Disorganized killer	67
Dodd, John Wesley	
Behavior reinforcement	137
Frontline quote	19
trophies	68
Drives, instinctual	11
Drug use	16

F

Fantasy	12, 23, 31, 54, 58, 115
Antecedent behavior as clue	135
Fantasy deviation	72
Fantasy, control	60
Fantasy, escalation	60
Fantasy, externalization	13-14
Fantasy, growth of	60
Fantasy, pattern	61
Fantasy, rehersal	35
Fantasy, reinforcement	13
FBI - VICAP	64

G

Gacy, John Wayne	
Manipulation	77
Graham, Harrison Drawings	65

H

Heidnik, Gary M.	
Constitution of church	143

Diagnosis, DSM	99
Drawing, basement	41
Drawing, basement killings	124
Fantasy and goal	76
Letter, basement killings	123
Letter, control	139
Letter, Davidson family	47
Letter, Davidson kidnapping	40
Letter, fantasy	32-37
Letter, financial investments	89
Letter, intimacy	117
Letter, Prenatal care	48
Letter, Sandra Lindsay death	55
Letter, social services	93
Letter, suicide 2/5/86	101
Letter, suicide February 1986	105
Letter, suicide, best attempt	109
Letter, suicide, last attempt	107
Letter, women	72
Manipulation when young	88
Manipulations, list	78
Mental health history	131
Motive	63
Personalities	45, 132
Previous kidnapping conviction	39
Real world ability	36
Serial murder, details	122
Statement to police, 3/25/87	80
Structured setting, the need for	88
Transcript, cross examination Davidson trial	188
Victim selection	69
Hooker, Cameron	28

I

Insane, ALI definition	2
Insane, legal definition	1
Insane, M'Naghten rule	1, 9
Intimacy	113, 116
Intimacy and control	21, 27

Serial killers	115
Intimacy and Control Theory	147
Intimacy, bonding, control - Serial killers	112

K

Kill, G.M. aka G.M. Heidnik	49, 131
Kool, Kenneth	22

L

Law enforcement	
Classic methods, why they don't work	136
Clues	115
Serial killer, apprehension	138
Victim commonalty	136
Leyton, Elliott	5

M

Malingering	79
Manipulation	75, 132
Manipulation and fantasy	77
Manipulation and suicide	101
Mass murderes, Categories	3
Masturbatory behavior	13
Mutilation 5	6

N

Norris, Joel	11
Mask of Sanity[a]	18

O

Organized crime killers	4
Organized killer	67

P

PA vs Gary M. Heidnik, 1988	9
Peruto, A. Charles, Jr.	23
Pornography	54
Power struggle with social services	92
Premeditation	35
Psychotic serial killer	4
Punishment, avoidance of	14

R

Rappaport, Richard	3
Ressler, Robert K.	31, 64
Serial killer behaviors	136
Ritual, compulsive	10
RSR mechanism	13

S

Serial killers

Ability to control real world	137
Behaviors	15
Categories	3
Characteristics	9
Childhood abuse	26

Definition	5
Diagnostic category	10
Family life	112
Functional analysis	135
Historical names	5
Inadequacy feelings	17
Intimacy - control conflicts	27,28,114
Internal struggle	20
Investigation of	64
Manipulation	17
Miscalculations of	76
Mode of murder, meaning	117
Modern day	6
Parental relationships	113
Ressler study results	12
Search for help	18
Self-manipulation	76
Sexual needs	58
Trophies	68
Sexual saddest serial killer	4
Suicide	22, 101
Control and manipulation	106

T

Thomas, Lisa	23, 69
Victim selection ritual	70
Tone of voice	169

V

Victim selection	63
apparent randomness	68
Common factors - Heidnik	71
Control ritual	71
Deviation from ritual	72
Fantasy	68
Ritual	69

Violent behavior predictors 15
Visions 16

W

Wolfgang, Marvin 26

Read the book that is the foundation of Probing the Mind of a Serial Killer

The Intimacy Manual:
Balancing Control and Intimacy in the Bedroom and the Boardroom

Edmund J. Amidon, Marilyn G. Amidon, Jack A. Apsche, Michael L. Silverman, and Eugene H. Stivers

ISBN 0-945510-08-X Paper (5-1/2 x 8-1/2)

1992 370 pages, indexed, illustrations, evaluation instruments.
$39.95

This landmark book was developed as a university level textbook and has become an indispensable reference for practicing psychologists all over the world. It is the result of decades of research at Temple University on human communication.

"Professional, well-written ... scientifically astute. The right stuff."

—*The Bookreader Magazine*

Use your VISA or MasterCard and

call 1/800-645-6973 or write:

International Information Associates, Inc.

P.O. Box 773, Morrisville, PA 19067-0773 USA